GENDER EQUALITY AND DISABILITY INCLUSION

GUIDELINES TO ADDRESS THE SPECIFIC NEEDS OF WOMEN AND GIRLS WITH DISABILITIES

MAY 2024

ASIAN DEVELOPMENT BANK

ADB

ADB Sector Guidelines

Health
Policy reforms to address the health and well-being of women and girls with disabilities

Education
Inclusive education, recognizing all learners have unique characteristics, interests, abilities, and particular learning needs

Social Protection
Consider the **basic cost** of living besides adequate health assistance and the costs of accessing reasonable accommodations

Water
Need for a dedicated focus addressing women and girls with disabilities in **water security**

Transport
Universal design for physical and sensory accessibility

Urban Development
Dedicated research to understand the multiple barriers facing women with disabilities in urban areas

ADDRESS THE WOMEN AND GIR

Govern
Disability inclusion in

Project Co
Budget for gendered disa
Needs assessment a

Project
Capacity building for
gender and disabilit

Monitorin
Specific indicators with outc

Decision-Making and Leadership

Only 4 countries had a woman with disabilities in national legislative bodies out of 18 countries researched in the Asia and Pacific region

Time Poverty and Drudgery Reduced

Women with disabilities are more likely to be engaged in unpaid work than women without disabilities

22% of women in lower-in
compare

GENDER AND DISABILITY INCLUSIVE DEVELOPMENT

...S TO

...CIFIC NEEDS OF
...ITH DISABILITIES

...ialogue
...y Partnership Strategy

...nd Design
...on aspects of the project
...r-disaggregated data

...entation
...and private sector on
...en with disabilities

...valuation
...men and girls with disabilities

Resilience to External Shocks Strengthened

Women with disabilities are disproportionately affected by the climate crisis, humanitarian crises, and the pandemic

Eliminating Harmful Social Norms and Practices

Women with disabilities experience intimate partner violence at a rate of 44% compared to 26% for women without disabilities

Economic Empowerment

Only 20% of women with disabilities are in paid employment

Women with disabilities earn on **average half** the income for similar jobs as men with disabilities

...countries have a disability
...% of men

© 2024 Asian Development Bank
6 ADB Avenue, Mandaluyong City, 1550 Metro Manila, Philippines
Tel +63 2 8632 4444; Fax +63 2 8636 2444
www.adb.org

Some rights reserved. Published in 2024.

ISBN 978-92-9270-649-4 (print); 978-92-9270-650-0 (PDF); 978-92-9270-651-7 (ebook)
Publication Stock No. TIM240217-2
DOI: http://dx.doi.org/10.22617/TIM240217-2

Note:
In this publication, "$" refers to United States dollars.

Cover design by Noelito Francisco Trivino.

Contents

Tables, Figures, and Boxes

Boxes

Foreword

An estimated 19% of women globally have a disability compared to 12% of men, with this increasing to 22.1% of women in lower-income countries.[1] Women and girls with disabilities face the same forms of discrimination and social disadvantage that nondisabled women and girls do, and face as well those faced by men and boys with disabilities. However, women with disabilities have a higher risk of having their sexual and reproductive rights curtailed, compared to women without disabilities, or men with disabilities. Women with disabilities have triple the illiteracy rate of men with disabilities and their health care needs are unmet. Additionally, they suffer double the unemployment rate and experience only half the amount of internet access.[2]

Building on the experience of the Asian Development Bank (ADB) as a strategic partner in social inclusion, social development, gender mainstreaming, and disability-inclusive development, these guidelines are aligned with the ADB *Strategy 2030 Operational Plan for Priority 2: Accelerating Progress in Gender Equality, 2019–2024*, Sustainable Development Goal 5 (SDG5) on gender quality and empowerment of women and girls, the Convention on the Rights of Persons with Disabilities, ADB's *Strengthening Disability-Inclusive Development,* and a chapter in *Deepening Civil Society Engagement for Disability-Inclusive Development Effectiveness in ADB Operations and the Disability Inclusion Brief* (Working title, Unpublished).

The guidelines were developed by the ADB Gender Equality Division in collaboration with the Social Development Team, Human and Social Development Sector Office, and are designed to assist ADB staff, government, and civil society development partners to strengthen an approach to gender- and disability-responsive development in the region. A specific sector focus has been used to address the needs, concerns, and empowerment of women and girls with disabilities in the infrastructure areas of water, sanitation, and hygiene (WASH); urban development and transport; as well as the social sectors of education, health, and social protection.

ADB is supporting several projects that pioneered some gender- and disability-inclusive responses to programming; and highlights the skills and leadership of women with disabilities. The Guidelines draw from this work including a lived experience case study regarding social protection in Tonga through the *Social Protection of the Vulnerable in the Pacific* project; an interview with the Peshawar organization of Persons with Disabilities on their involvement in the project *Trans Peshawar Bus Transport System*

---

1   CBM. 2019. *Leave No One Behind: Gender Equality, Disability Inclusion and Leadership for Sustainable Development.* Melbourne: CBM. p. 3; and World Health Organization and the World Bank. 2011. *World Report on Disability.* Geneva: WHO. p. 28.

2   UN. 2020. *Sixth Session of the Working Group on the Asian and Pacific Decade of Persons with Disabilities, 2013–2022: Review of Recent Progress in the Implementation of the Asian and Pacific Decade of Persons with Disabilities, 2013–2022.* Bangkok: UN Economic and Social Commission for Asia and the Pacific.

in Pakistan, and a case study looking at gender- and disability-responsive features of urban planning in Georgia through the initiative *Fair Shared Green and Recreational Spaces Guidelines for Gender-Responsive and Inclusive Design.*

The guidelines were developed to provide a broad overview of the nexus of gender inequality and disability exclusion and to emphasize the approach of "nothing about us without us." The resource draws from and advocates for engagement with diverse groups of women with different types of disabilities and organizations of persons with disabilities to ensure their voices and lived experiences are recognized, respected, and incorporated into designs and strategic interventions.

We hope the insights that this publication offers will foster learning, dialogue, and innovative approaches to address the needs and empowerment of women and girls with disabilities in our developing member countries.

These guidelines represent a significant step forward in ADB's work dedicated to gender- and disability-responsive development. We thank everyone who contributed their guidance, expertise, and commitment to help create it.

BRUNO CARRASCO
Director General
Climate Change and Sustainable Development Department
Asian Development Bank

Acknowledgments

The Gender Equality and Disability Inclusion: Guidelines to Address the Specific Needs of Women and Girls with Disabilities (2023) to address the specific needs of women and girls with disabilities was drafted by Suzette Mitchell, a woman with disabilities, under the guidance of Prabhjot Khan, senior Social Development specialist (Gender and Development), Gender Equality Division (CCGE), Climate Change and Sustainable Development Department (CCSD), and Claire Charamnac, Social Development specialist (Gender and Development), Gender Equality Division (CCGE), Climate Change and Sustainable Development Department (CCSD). Thank you to Samantha Hung, director, Gender Equality Division (CCGE), Climate Change and Sustainable Development Department (CCSD) for her guidance throughout the development of the draft and Wendy Walker, director, Social Development Team, Human and Social Development Sector Office, Sectors Group (SG-HSD), who provided technical advice in the development of the publication.

The draft was extensively peer reviewed by development partners, civil society organizations, ADB staff, which included women with disabilities: Dwi Ariyani, regional head of Programs-Asia Disability Rights Fund; Rosario Galarza, Intersectionalities officer, International Disability Alliance; Pratima Gurung, general secretary for Indigenous Persons with Disabilities Global Network, chair of the National Indigenous Disabled Women Association, Nepal, and board member, Women Enabled International; Alisa Sivathorn, Disability Inclusion and Empowerment specialist, United Nations Development Programme (UNDP), Bangkok Regional Hub; Andrea Cole, director, and Rowena Harbridge, assistant director, Disability Equity and Rights, Department of Foreign Affairs and Trade (DFAT); Teresa Lee, Disability Inclusion adviser and Aleisha Caroll, manager, Inclusion Advisor of CBM Australia—all provided extremely useful feedback as external peer reviewers. Malika Shagazatova, senior Social Development specialist, CCGE, and Joanna Rogers, Social Protection specialist (consultant), SG-HSD of ADB, peer reviewed the draft and provided invaluable guidance.

Other staff from various departments, including Lloyd Frederick Wright, senior Urban Development specialist (Transport), Transport Sector Office; Ninebeth Carandang, principal Social Development specialist, SG-HSD; and Francesco Tornieri, principal Social Development specialist (Gender and Development), SG-HSD, provided helpful suggestions during consultations.

We are thankful for the support of Nicholas Booth, programme adviser, Governance, Conflict Prevention, Access to Justice and Human Rights, UNDP, Bangkok Regional Hub; Jacqueline de Rose-Ahern, assistant director, Human Rights Policy and Social Inclusion Branch, Disability, Indigenous Issues and Social Inclusion Section, DFAT; and Aiko Akiyama, Disability manager, Social Development Unit, *Economic and Social Commission for Asia and the Pacific (ESCAP)*.

We appreciate the support of **civil society organizations** for participating in interviews and consultations: Mikaela Patrick, senior Inclusive Design researcher, Global Disability Innovation Hub; Chanhpheng Sivila, director, Lao Women with Disability Association; Shahab Ud Din, chief executive officer of Pak Everbright Development Organization (PEDO); Saphia Grant, former project manager, Asia Pacific Gender with Disability Network, Women with Disabilities Australia (WWDA).

Monina M. Gamboa edited *The Gender Equality and Disability Inclusion: Guidelines to Address the Specific Needs of Women and Girls with Disabilities* (2023). Noelito Francisco Trivinio designed the cover, Jonathan P. Yamongan designed the layout and Keisuke Taketani created graphics used in this publication.

Abbreviations

ADB	Asian Development Bank
CEDAW	Convention on the Elimination of All Forms of Discrimination against Women
COVID-19	coronavirus disease
CRPD	Convention on the Rights of Persons with Disabilities
CSO	civil society organization
DFAT	Department of Foreign Affairs and Trade (Australia)
DMC	developing member country
ESCAP	Economic and Social Commission for Asia and the Pacific
FCDO	Foreign, Commonwealth and Development Office (United Kingdom)
GBV	gender-based violence
GLAD	Global Action on Disability
IDA	International Disability Alliance
IPWDGN	Indigenous Persons with Disabilities Global Network
NGO	nongovernment organization
NIDWAN	National Indigenous Disabled Women Association
OECD DAC	Organisation for Economic Co-operation and Development's Development Assistance Committee
OP1	ADB's Strategy 2030 Operational Plan for Priority 1: Addressing Remaining Poverty and Reducing Inequalities
OP2	ADB's Strategy 2030 Operational Plan for Priority 2: Accelerating Progress in Gender Equality
OPD	Organization of Persons with Disabilities
SADD	sex, age, and disability disaggregated data
SDG	Sustainable Development Goal
SOGIESC	sexual orientation, gender identity, gender expression, and sex characteristics
SRH	sexual and reproductive health

TVET	technical and vocational education and training
UN	United Nations
UNDP	United Nations Development Programme
UN Women	United Nations Entity for Gender Equality and the Empowerment of Women
VAW	violence against women
WASH	water, sanitation, and hygiene
WGQ	Washington Group Questions
WHO	World Health Organization

1 Introduction

The World Health Organization (WHO) estimates that persons with disabilities comprise 16% of the world's population,[1] with 70% or around 690 million of these people living in the Asia and Pacific region. An estimated 19% of women globally have a disability compared to 12% of men, with this increasing to 22.1% of women in lower-income countries.[2] This discrepancy is partly due to women living longer and becoming disabled from the impacts of gender inequality in health access and gender-based violence (GBV).

Persons with disabilities and their families are at risk of experiencing higher levels of poverty and unemployment and lower levels of education and poorer health. This risk is elevated for women and girls with disabilities who experience gender inequality, sexism, and stereotyping alongside ableism, disability exclusion, and expectations to conform to specific social and ethnic cultural norms. Women and girls with disabilities experience direct and indirect discrimination; historical, structural, and systemic discrimination; as well as associative discrimination (such as when employers perceive women with disabilities will be less productive when they are carers of family members with disabilities). The intersection of these forms of discrimination compounds the impact of these inequalities and creates additional, unique barriers for women and girls with disabilities. For example, compared with women without disabilities or men with disabilities, women with disabilities are more likely to experience the violation of their sexual and reproductive health rights, including forced sterilization, abortion, or contraception.[3] In addition, women with disabilities have triple the illiteracy rate and double the unemployment rate of men with disabilities.

While the coronavirus disease (COVID-19) has not created the inequalities that women with disabilities experience, it has exacerbated many elements of gender inequality and disability exclusion. This has led to increased health risks (especially for women with disabilities who are immunocompromised), as well as social exclusion due to lockdowns which have also contributed to a global increase in GBV due to women's close confinement with their partners (footnote 5).

Women and girls with disabilities, and persons with disabilities who are also of diverse sexual orientation, gender identity, social, economic, and ethnic identity gender expression, and sex characteristics (SOGIESC) have diverse identities and types of impairment, which necessitates nuanced approaches to addressing their marginalization. For example, the specific context for an illiterate blind woman from an ethnic group in a remote area of Viet Nam will differ significantly from a

---

[1] World Health Organization. 7 March 2023. Disability (who.int).

[2] CBM. 2019. *Leave No One Behind: Gender Equality, Disability Inclusion and Leadership for Sustainable Development*. Melbourne: CBM. p. 3; and World Health Organization and the World Bank. 2011. *World Report on Disability*. Geneva: WHO. p. 28.

[3] Further forms of gender-based violence inflicted against women with disabilities are discussed in section 2.

woman with cognitive impairments in Suva, the capital city of Fiji. These guidelines provide an analysis of core barriers faced by the majority of women and girls with disabilities throughout the Asia and Pacific region. This includes strategies to address their needs, especially in the context of poverty, while considering the additional complexity faced by groups of women and girls with diverse forms of disability (e.g., indigenous or older women with disabilities). The Convention on the Rights of Persons with Disabilities (CRPD) states that disability is an evolving concept[4] and refers to persons with disabilities in Article 1 as including those who have "long-term physical, mental, intellectual, or sensory impairments which in interaction with various barriers may hinder their full and effective participation in society on an equal basis with others." These forms of disability are referred to throughout these guidelines as physical, sensory, cognitive, and psychosocial.

Historically, the disability inclusion sector has not overtly focused on women with disabilities, and women's groups have not been sufficiently disability inclusive,[5] however, this is changing. The focus of work addressing issues faced by women and girls with disabilities has been in GBV, sexual and reproductive health rights, leadership, decision-making, and employment.

To date, many women and girls with disabilities have been marginalized and made invisible in mainstream development policies and programs, however, local and international groups of women with disabilities have used their lived experience to advocate for change. These groups have called for a strength-based approach that recognizes the potential of women with disabilities as active citizens, rather than viewing them as passive victims in the community. For women and girls with disabilities, as for all persons with disabilities, the preferred approach is a transition from a deficit medical model that predominantly considers their impairments to a social and rights-based model of inclusivity that identifies the societal barriers that prevent their active participation in society. This requires the implementation of reasonable accommodations and universal design in physical spaces, as well as addressing attitudinal and enabling safe spaces, legal and economic barriers, and access to information.

A human rights-based approach ensures the empowerment of women and girls with disabilities and promotes their active role in decision-making and autonomy in all aspects of their lives and society. This entails addressing legislative frameworks, societal attitudes, and full and equal access to all—education, health, and social services—informed specifically by women with disabilities themselves. Consultation with organizations of persons with disabilities (OPDs), especially those run by and for women—or at a minimum, those with a dedicated focus on gender in disability inclusion—is a critical first step to ensure development initiatives meet the needs of women and girls with disabilities. "Nothing about us without us" is the motto of the disability movement. This set of guidelines was developed by a woman with disabilities and has been peer reviewed by several women with disabilities active in the sector and is supplemented by case studies of lived experience.

For all key terms related to disability inclusion and gender equality, see the glossary in Appendix 1. For a full outline of the concepts used in disability inclusion for all persons with disabilities, see the ADB resources: *Deepening Civil Society Engagement for Disability-Inclusive Development Effectiveness in ADB Operations* (Working title. Unpublished) and the *Disability Inclusion Brief* (Working title. Unpublished).

---

[4]   CRPD preamble, para. (iii).
[5]   UN Women. 2020. *Addressing exclusion through intersectionality in rule of law, peace and security context.* New York: UN Women, p. 2.

2 Purpose, Outline, and Scope of the Guidelines

The purpose of these guidelines is to inform developing member country (DMC) officials, practitioners, clients, and ADB staff on key issues that create barriers for women and girls with disabilities in development programs, as well as provide an understanding of strategies to empower women with disabilities in their roles as community members, family members, workers, and leaders in all aspects of society. The guidelines were developed through a desk review and a set of interviews with ADB staff and external stakeholders from organizations working in the disability and gender inclusion space. This included speaking to women with lived experience of diverse forms of disability in the Asia and Pacific region.

The publication begins with outlining the ADB *Strengthening Disability-Inclusive Development, 2021–2025 Road Map,* followed by a summary of the key international United Nations guiding documents that specifically refer to women and girls with disabilities. The guidelines outline the central issues addressing the intersection of gender and disability, which result in multiple marginalization of women and girls with disabilities. An intersectionality approach is then used to recognize the additional and specific issues for diverse women and girls with disabilities to "leave no one behind." An analysis of key issues facing women and girls with disabilities is outlined according to the priorities identified in ADB's *Strategy 2030 Operational Plan for Priority 2: Accelerating Progress in Gender Equality, 2019–2024* (OP2). These are women's economic empowerment, gender equality in human development, decision-making and leadership, women's time poverty, and women's resilience to external shocks, as well as an alignment with the Sustainable Development Goal (SDG) on gender equality and the empowerment of all women and girls.

The publication is designed to be practical with an outline of critical issues to address for women and girls with disabilities across all development work. A range of sectors is then identified to provide a more detailed and systematic approach to a gendered disability inclusion approach in projects and program design, implementation, monitoring, and review. Sector guidelines are provided for the infrastructure sectors of water, sanitation, and hygiene, urban development, and transport, as well as the social sectors of education, health, and social protection. Each sector guideline includes an outline of key issues and barriers faced by women and girls with disabilities in the sector and suggested entry points to enable them to access the appropriate forms of assistance and to fully participate in development programming to ensure their voices and lived experience are recognized, respected, and incorporated into designs and strategic interventions. This is supplemented with a checklist and set of indicators specifically developed to measure the outcomes of programming for women and girls with disabilities, ensuring the collection of sex, age, and disability data along with other key measures. Case studies in each sector highlight real-life issues drawn from the voices of women throughout Asia and the Pacific. Additionally, a set of relevant and useful resources are provided at the end of each sector.

3 The Role of the Asian Development Bank

Strategy 2030 sets out the mandate of the Asian Development Bank (ADB) to expand its vision to achieve a prosperous, inclusive, resilient, and sustainable Asia and Pacific region, while sustaining efforts to eradicate extreme poverty. In 2019, ADB approved operational plans for its seven operational priorities under Strategy 2030, including Operational Priority (OP) 1: Addressing Remaining Poverty and Reducing Inequalities 2019–2024 (OP1) and OP2. While OP1 recognizes addressing disability inclusion, OP2 recognizes the importance of gender equality in its own right as well as for helping achieve gender-inclusive socioeconomic development, and is fully aligned with the 2030 Agenda for Sustainable Development, which ADB and its members have committed to support. OP2 highlights the importance of considering the intersectionality between gender equality and other axes of discrimination, including those related to disability, and commits to identifying and addressing these multiple discriminations and vulnerabilities.

In 2021, ADB approved a *Strengthening Disability-Inclusive Development, 2021–2025 Road Map*. This publication sets out a practical route to greater disability inclusion in ADB projects, research, organizational systems, and collaboration with OPDs. This recognizes the specific and gender- and disability-based discrimination faced by women and girls with disabilities, as expressed in Box 1.

Box 1: Strengthening Disability-Inclusive Development, 2021–2025 Road Map

In most areas of life, women and girls face many barriers resulting from the interplay between poverty and gender- and disability-based discrimination, which hinder access to equal opportunities for education, employment, and social interaction. Vulnerability to violence also increases significantly, especially among women with intellectual disabilities.

Source: Asian Development Bank. 2022. *Strengthening Disability-Inclusive Development 2021–2025 Road Map*. Manila: ADB.

A specific component of the road map is to develop sector guidelines and gradually expand a portfolio of disability-inclusive development interventions. As such, this publication addresses the commitment to develop guidelines on gender and disability inclusion to recognize the challenges for women and girls with disabilities.

ADB has pioneered some gender- and disability-inclusive responses to programming in the areas of education, social protection, urban planning, and transportation that will be featured throughout these guidelines. The Asian Development Bank Institute has also dedicated specific research into the needs of women with disabilities in a Working Paper on *Entrepreneurship Training and Online Marketplace Participation among Female Persons with Disabilities.*[6]

New resources from ADB include the *Disability Inclusion Brief* and *Deepening Civil Society Engagement for Disability-Inclusive Development Effectiveness in ADB Operations* (unpublished). Both these publications provide a thorough outline of disability inclusion processes for all persons with disabilities for ADB staff and sector partners. They are companion publications to this set of guidelines, supplementing the broader approach to disability inclusion in development. *Deepening Civil Society Engagement for Disability-Inclusive Development Effectiveness in ADB Operations* provides an extensive outline on OPDs in the region, how to engage with them, and includes an OPD assessment tool. The ADB *Disability Inclusion Brief* includes a language guide for referring to persons with disabilities, a full overview of internal and regional policies and commitments, and a guide to addressing disability inclusion throughout the country partnership strategy, as well as the wider program development process.

ADB is an active member of the Global Action on Disability Network (GLAD) which brings together stakeholders from governments, United Nations (UN) agencies, bilateral and multilateral banks, and public and private organizations working on disability inclusion and the rights of persons with disabilities, as well as the GLAD Gender Equality Working Group. The GLAD Working Group was formed to address the invisibility of women and girls with disabilities within both the disability and women's movements. One of the principles of this working group is to break down siloes that exist within institutions and the donor community between gender and disability. This resource represents an action on behalf of ADB to fulfill this principle.

---

[6]   S. W. Gan et al. 2022. *Entrepreneurship Training and Online Marketplace Participation among Female Persons with Disabilities.* ADBI Working Paper 1342. Tokyo: Asian Development Bank Institute.

4 International and Regional Normative Frameworks

Over several decades, the UN has led national governments and global stakeholders to make commitments to address the human rights of women, girls, and people of diverse SOGIESC with disabilities. Some of these commitments are included below, noting these are limited to those that specifically address women and girls with disabilities. There are many more core international documents that address disability inclusion and gender separately.

4.1 The Convention on the Rights of Persons with Disabilities

The *Convention on the Rights of Persons with Disabilities* (CRPD) is seen as a global standard setting framework to address the rights of persons with disabilities. It defines key terms and concepts that are critical to the sector and can be found in Appendix 1. These definitions include discrimination, disability, universal design, reasonable accommodation, and communication.

Article 6 of CRPD recognizes the vulnerability of women and girls with disabilities, and sets provisions and measures for state parties to follow to ensure they are empowered and can participate fully in society:

> The CPRD Optional Protocol on the situation of women and girls with disabilities, focuses on a number of key issues critical to realizing the rights of women and girls with disabilities on the equal basis with others, namely multiple and intersecting forms of discrimination; education and employment; access to health services, including sexual and reproductive health; access to justice and equal recognition before the law; and participation in public and political life. Article 6 on women and girls with disabilities recognizes the multiple forms of discrimination faced by women and girls with disabilities, and calls for the full development, advancement and empowerment of women with disabilities.[7]

In 2016, the Committee on the Rights of Persons with Disabilities released General Comment No. 3 on women and girls with disabilities. This is the core UN document dedicated specifically to obligations of national governments to the rights of women and girls with disabilities. As such, this document is referenced significantly throughout this set of guidelines as a globally agreed-on and standard-setting reference.

---

[7] UN General Assembly. 2017. *Implementation of the Convention on the Rights of Persons with Disabilities and the Optional Protocol thereto: situation of women and girls with disabilities: resolution/adopted by the General Assembly (A/RES/72/162).* New York: UNGA.

Core definitions from the Convention on the Rights of Persons with Disabilities, Article 2

> **"Communication"** includes languages, display of text, Braille, tactile communication, large print, accessible multimedia, as well as written, audio, plain-language, human-reader, and augmentative and alternative modes, means, and formats of communication, including accessible information and communication technology.
>
> **"Language"** includes spoken and signed languages and other forms of non-spoken languages.

> **"Discrimination on the basis of disability"** means any distinction, exclusion, or restriction on the basis of disability which has the purpose or effect of impairing or nullifying the recognition, enjoyment, or exercise, on an equal basis with others, of all human rights and fundamental freedoms in the political, economic, social, cultural, civil, or any other field. It includes all forms of discrimination, including denial of reasonable accommodation.

> **"Reasonable accommodation"** means necessary and appropriate modification and adjustments not imposing a disproportionate or undue burden, where needed in a particular case, to ensure to persons with disabilities the enjoyment or exercise on an equal basis with others of all human rights and fundamental freedoms.

> **"Universal design"** means the design of products, environments, programs, and services to be usable by all people, to the greatest extent possible, without the need for adaptation or specialized design. Universal design shall not exclude assistive devices for particular groups of persons with disabilities where this is needed.

CRPD General Comment No. 5 (2017) on the right to live independently and being included in the community

The document states that any people with disabilities are presumed to be unable to live independently in their self-chosen communities due to support being unavailable or infrastructure is not universally designed, which has led to abandonment, dependence on family, institutionalization, isolation, and segregation (Article 1). Several sections of the document refer specifically to the exacerbated needs and risks for women and girls with disabilities in their pace of residence, especially institutions. Para. 72 states that women and girls with disabilities are:

> ... more excluded and isolated and face more restrictions regarding their place of residence as well as their living arrangements owing to paternalistic stereotyping and patriarchal social patterns that discriminate against women in society. Women and girls with disabilities also experience gender-based, multiple and intersectional discrimination, greater risk of institutionalization and violence, including sexual violence, abuse and harassment ...

Para. 83 further states:

> It is of paramount significance to ensure that support services leave no space for potential abuse or exploitation of persons with disabilities or any violence against them. Since institutions tend to isolate those who reside within them from the rest of the community, institutionalized women and girls with disabilities are further susceptible to gender-based violence, including forced sterilization, sexual and physical abuse, emotional abuse, and further isolation. They also face increased barriers to reporting such violence.

4.2   United Nations Fourth World Conference on Women Beijing Declaration and Platform for Action, 1995

The *Beijing Platform for Action* mainstreams the needs and concerns of women and girls with disabilities as a category of women and girls who face multiple barriers across the 12 critical areas of concern.[8] Additionally, specific paragraphs are dedicated to the specific needs of women and girls with disabilities in the areas of women and health, violence against women, women and the economy, institutional mechanisms for the advancement of women, and human rights of women and the girl child. These stress the need to ensure that girls and women of all ages with any form of disability receive supportive services; access to information and services in the field of violence against women; special programs to enable them to obtain and retain employment, access to education and training at all proper levels, adjusted working conditions and legal protection against unfounded job loss on account of their disabilities; improve data collection on the participation of women and girls with disabilities, including their access to resources; ensure nondiscrimination and equal enjoyment of all human rights and fundamental freedoms by women and girls with disabilities, including their access to information and services in the field of violence against women, as well as their active participation in and economic contribution to all aspects of society; publicize and disseminate information in easily understandable formats and alternative formats appropriate for disabilities, and low levels of literacy; and ensure equal provision of appropriate services and devices to girls with disabilities, and provide their families with related support services.

4.3   The Convention on the Elimination of All Forms of Discrimination against Women

While the *Convention on the Elimination of All Forms of Discrimination against Women* (CEDAW) does not explicitly refer to women and girls with disabilities, the General Recommendation of the Committee on the Elimination of Discrimination Against Women No. 18 in 2006 notes that women with disabilities are doubly marginalized and recognizes the scarcity of data, and calls on States parties to provide this information in their periodic reports and ensure the participation of women and girls with disabilities in all areas of social and cultural life. In 2019, a joint general recommendation

---

[8]   The 12 critical areas of the Platform for Action are: (1) women and poverty; (2) education and training of women; (3) women and health; (4) violence against women; (5) women and armed conflict; (6) women and the economy; (7) women in power and decision-making; (8) institutional mechanisms; (9) human rights of women; (10) women and media; (11) women and the environment; (12) the girl child.

was endorsed by the CEDAW committee (No. 31) and the Convention on the Rights of the Child Committee (No. 18) on Harmful Practices. The recommendation refers to harmful practices strongly connected to socially constructed gender roles, and systems of patriarchal power relations and negative perceptions of or discriminatory beliefs regarding certain disadvantaged groups of women and children, including individuals with disabilities or albinism.

CEDAW General Recommendation No. 39 (2022) on the rights of Indigenous women and girls

This recommendation identifies and addresses different forms of intersectional discrimination for indigenous women which are identified as including "racism, racial discrimination, and the effects of colonialism; sex- and gender-based discrimination; discrimination on the basis of socioeconomic status; disability-based discrimination; barriers in gaining access to their lands, territories, and natural resources; the lack of adequate and culturally pertinent health and education services; and disruptions and threats to their spiritual lives."[9] The recommendation also identifies that indigenous women and girls with disabilities often face the arbitrary removal and abduction of their children. It highlights the gravity of discrimination and GBV against indigenous women and girls with disabilities who are living in institutions and the denial of their legal capacity, which leads to further human rights violations, including in the areas of access to justice, institutionalized violence, and forced sterilization.

4.4   Convention on the Rights of the Child

In 2006, the Committee on the Rights of the Child specifically addressed the rights of children with disabilities. Gender discrimination was identified as making girls with disabilities more vulnerable to discrimination, with States parties requested to take necessary measures, and when needed, extra measures, to ensure that girls with disabilities are well protected, have access to all services, and are fully included in society. The Committee raised the practice of forced sterilization of children with disabilities—particularly girls with disabilities—recognizing this still-present practice seriously violates the child's physical integrity and results in lifelong physical and mental health effects. The Committee urged States parties to prohibit the forced sterilization of children with disabilities by law. Refugee and internally displaced girls with disabilities were also identified as more at risk of abuse, including sexual abuse, neglect, and exploitation.[10]

4.5   The 2030 Agenda for Sustainable Development

The *2030 Agenda for Sustainable Development* highlights the crosscutting nature of gender and disability issues, building on the principle of "leaving no one behind." The approach recognizes the systematic mainstreaming of gender-based perspectives across all the sustainable development goals SDGs and targets and calls for the empowerment of persons with disabilities. The 2030 Agenda has a stand-alone goal on gender equality and the empowerment of all women and girls (SDG5) and includes persons with disabilities in the SDGs related to poverty, hunger education, WASH, economic

---

[9]   See A/HRC/EMRIP/2014/3/Rev.1. paras 35–42; and Inter-American Commission on Human Rights, *Indigenous Women and their Human Rights in the Americas.* OEA/Ser.L/V/II. Doc. 44/17. para. 138.

[10]   UN Committee on the Rights of the Child. 2006. General Comment No. 9 (2006): *The rights of children with disabilities.* Geneva: CRC.

growth and employment, inequality, accessibility of human settlements, climate change, and data, monitoring, and accountability. SDG Goals 1, 4, 5, 8, 10, 11, and 16 refer to the need for both gender and disability data, however, the connection between gender and disability is not a specific focus.

4.6   Incheon Strategy to "Make the Right Real" for Persons with Disabilities in Asia and the Pacific, 2012

Article 3 of the *Beijing Declaration, including the Action Plan to Accelerate the Implementation of the Incheon Strategy*[11] refers to the Sendai Framework for Disaster Risk Reduction 2015–2030 and states:

> … the importance of empowering persons with disabilities to publicly lead and promote universally accessible response, recovery, rehabilitation, and reconstruction approaches in disaster risk reduction, and of applying the principles of universal design to strengthening disaster-resilient public and private investments in disaster risk prevention and reduction.

Goal 6 of the Incheon Strategy seeks to ensure gender equality and women's empowerment (Box 2). There are four specific targets under the goal:

- Enable women and girls with disabilities to have equitable access to mainstream development opportunities,
- Ensure representation of women with disabilities in government decision-making bodies,
- Ensure that all women and girls with disabilities have access to sexual and reproductive health services on an equitable basis with girls and women without disabilities, and
- Increase measures to protect women and girls with disabilities from all forms of violence and abuse.

Box 2: Incheon Strategy to "Make the Right Real" for Persons with Disabilities in Asia and the Pacific

Goal 6: Ensure gender equality and women's empowerment.

Girls and women with disabilities face multiple forms of discrimination and abuse. Isolation, compounded by dependency on caregivers, renders them extremely vulnerable to many forms of exploitation, violence, and abuse, with attendant risks, including of human immunodeficiency virus (HIV) infection, pregnancy, and maternal and infant death. Girls and women with disabilities are largely invisible in mainstream gender equality programs. Information concerning sexual and reproductive health, general health care, and related services is seldom in formats and language that are accessible. The true promise of the decade will be fully realized only when girls and women with disabilities are active participants in mainstream development.

Source: UN ESCAP. 2018. *Building Disability-Inclusive Societies in Asia and the Pacific: Assessing Progress of the Incheon Strategy*. Bangkok: ESCAP.

---

[11]   Economic and Social Commission for Asia and the Pacific High-Level Intergovernmental Meeting on the Midpoint Review of the Asian and Pacific Decade of Persons with Disabilities, 2013–2022. Beijing, 27 November–1 December 2017. *Beijing Declaration, including the Action Plan to Accelerate the Implementation of the Incheon Strategy.*

4.7   The Charter and Guidelines on Inclusion of Persons with Disabilities in Humanitarian Action

The *Charter on Inclusion of Persons with Disabilities in Humanitarian Action* was launched at the 2016 World Humanitarian Summit by a coalition of member states, UN agencies, OPDs, international organizations, and civil society organizations. It calls for the empowerment and protection of women with disabilities from physical, sexual, and other forms of violence, abuse, exploitation, and harassment and commits to collecting data on persons with disabilities disaggregated by age and sex.

In 2019, the Humanitarian Coordination Inter-Agency Standing Committee (IASC) Reference Group on Inclusion of Persons with Disabilities in Humanitarian Action published a set of *Guidelines on Inclusion of Persons with Disabilities in Humanitarian Action*. The guidelines highlight that children with disabilities are at a higher risk of abuse and neglect, and women with disabilities are at a higher risk of sexual violence during humanitarian crises. A dedicated section of these guidelines deals with GBV and addresses the increased risk due to the intersection of socioeconomic stress, gender inequality, age, and disability issues. It states humanitarian actors and local authorities may not believe the reports of violence from women and girls with disabilities. The guide suggests these personnel as well as GBV staff should be trained on attitudes and assumptions about women and girls with disabilities with women-led OPDs specifically trained in how to safely identify and refer GBV survivors.[12]

4.8   2016–2025 Pacific Framework for the Rights of Persons with Disabilities

The *2016–2025 Pacific Framework for the Rights of Persons with Disabilities* identifies women with disabilities as a particularly vulnerable group. An outcome specifically addresses the need for women with disabilities to be appointed to leadership positions within government ministries, private sector organizations, OPDs, and civil society organizations.

4.9   The Beijing Declaration, including the Action Plan to Accelerate the Implementation of the Incheon Strategy, 2017

The Beijing Declaration further recommends governments to take the following actions to achieve Goal 6 of the Incheon Strategy: (a) accord priority to incorporating the perspectives of women and girls with disabilities in developing and implementing national action plans, legislation, and programs on gender equality and women's empowerment; and (b) disseminate information and enhance knowledge on comprehensive sexual and reproductive health and reproductive rights, as well as on the protection of women and girls with disabilities from violence, abuse, and exploitation.

---

12   IASC Task Team on inclusion of Persons with Disabilities in Humanitarian Action. 2019. *IASC Guidelines Inclusion of Persons with Disabilities in Humanitarian Action*. pp. 149–150. https://interagencystandingcommittee.org/system/files/2020-11/IASC%20 Guidelines%20on%20the%20Inclusion%20of%20Persons%20with%20Disabilities%20in%20Humanitarian%20 Action%2C%202019_0.pdf.

4.10 Jakarta Declaration on the Asian and Pacific Decade of Persons with Disabilities, 2023–2032

The Jakarta Declaration makes special mention of issues related to aging and gender, as well as a specific focus on gender within paragraph (16e) which states:

> Promote a gender-responsive life-cycle approach to developing and implementing disability-related policies and programs, paying particular attention to: (iv) responding to discrimination and barriers that women and girls with disabilities, including older women with disabilities, often face in terms of participation and of gaining access to information and services, including sexual and reproductive health services. (para. 16e)

All these official UN commitments indicate a growing recognition of issues faced by women and girls with disabilities with an international call to action. However, the UN has also stated that: "Despite these political commitments, women and girls with disabilities are often invisible in national laws and policies, and their meaningful participation remains marginal to global efforts to accelerate actions to advance the rights of women and girls with disabilities."[13]

---

[13]   UN. 2020. *Sixth session of the Working Group on the Asian and Pacific Decade of Persons with Disabilities, 2013–2022: Review of Recent Progress in the Implementation of the Asian and Pacific Decade of Persons with Disabilities, 2013–2022.* Bangkok: UN Economic and Social Commission for Asia and the Pacific.

5 Analysis of Issues Facing Women and Girls with Disabilities

5.1 What Lies at the Intersection of Gender Inequality and Disability Exclusion?

Women and girls with disabilities face the impacts of gender inequality and sexism, as well as disability exclusion and ableism. These structural inequalities create barriers to education, employment, and public and political life, which can lead to increases in poverty and vulnerability to violence, particularly for women and girls with intellectual disabilities.[14] These structural inequalities are often exacerbated in times of disaster, such as during the coronavirus disease (COVID-19) pandemic.[15]

To ensure women and girls with disabilities are not left behind in the development process, it is critical to identify the diverse barriers preventing their active and equitable inclusion in a life free from poverty and violence. However, the development sector must avoid viewing women and girls with disabilities through a deficit medical model that only considers their impairments, and shift to accommodate their needs and dismantle discrimination to enable their active participation and to amplify their voices in society (Box 3).

Box 3: Disability-Inclusive Development

Disability-inclusive development promotes effective development by recognizing that, like all members of a population, people with disabilities are both beneficiaries and agents of development. An inclusive approach seeks to identify and address barriers that prevent people with disabilities from participating in and benefiting from development. The explicit inclusion of people with disabilities as active participants in development processes leads to broader benefits for families and communities, reduces the impacts of poverty, and positively contributes to a country's economic growth.

Source: DFAT. 2015. *Development for All 2015–2020 Strategy for Strengthening Disability-Inclusive Development in Australia's Aid Program.* Canberra: DFAT. p. 7.

---

[14] DFAT. 2015. *Development for All 2015–2020: Strategy for Strengthening Disability-Inclusive Development in Australia's Aid Program.* Extended to 2021. Canberra: DFAT. Quoted in ADB. 2022. *Strengthening Disability-Inclusive Development 2021–2025 Road Map.* Manila: ADB.
[15] UN Women and Sightsavers. 2021. *"This virus has changed us all": Experiences of Women with Disabilities in the Asia-Pacific Region during COVID-19.* New York: UN Women.

Figure 1: The Nexus of Disability Exclusion and Gender Inequality

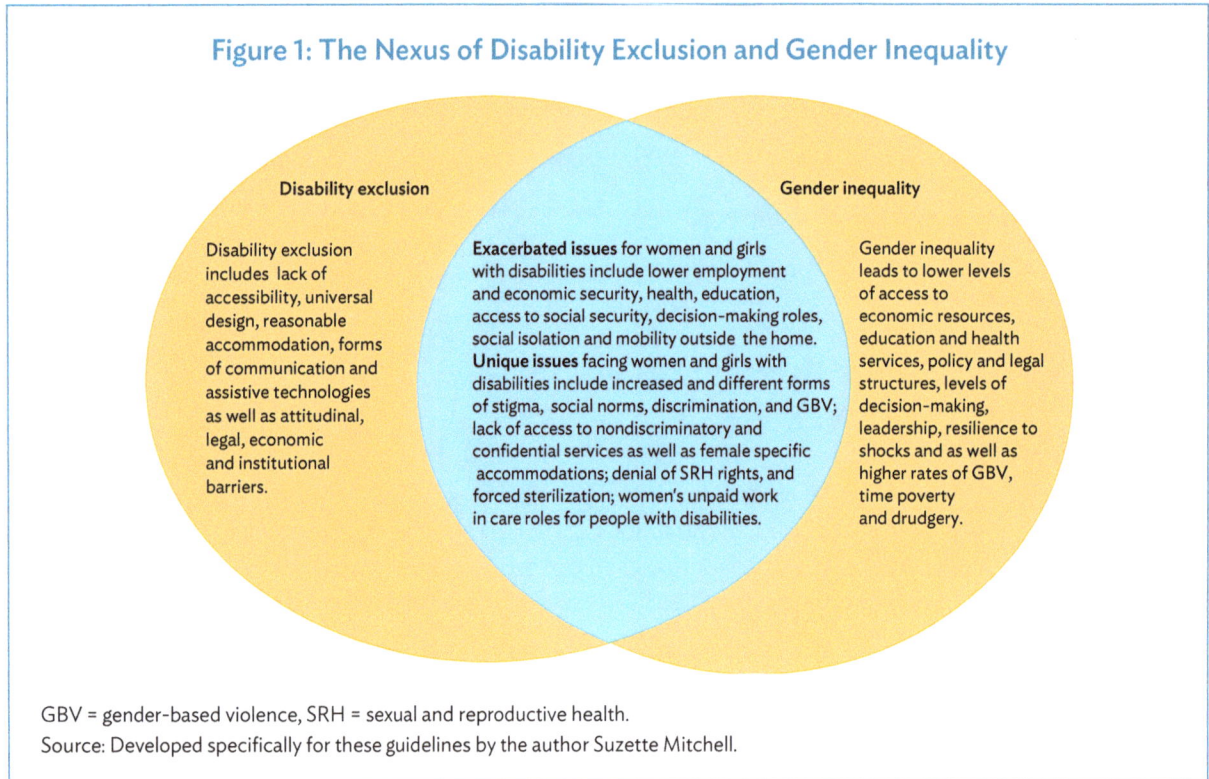

Disability exclusion

Disability exclusion includes lack of accessibility, universal design, reasonable accommodation, forms of communication and assistive technologies as well as attitudinal, legal, economic and institutional barriers.

Exacerbated issues for women and girls with disabilities include lower employment and economic security, health, education, access to social security, decision-making roles, social isolation and mobility outside the home. **Unique issues** facing women and girls with disabilities include increased and different forms of stigma, social norms, discrimination, and GBV; lack of access to nondiscriminatory and confidential services as well as female specific accommodations; denial of SRH rights, and forced sterilization; women's unpaid work in care roles for people with disabilities.

Gender inequality

Gender inequality leads to lower levels of access to economic resources, education and health services, policy and legal structures, levels of decision-making, leadership, resilience to shocks and as well as higher rates of GBV, time poverty and drudgery.

GBV = gender-based violence, SRH = sexual and reproductive health.
Source: Developed specifically for these guidelines by the author Suzette Mitchell.

Image description: A Venn diagram showing two intersecting circles, one labeled disability exclusion and the other labeled gender inequality. The area of intersection lists exacerbated and unique issues for women and girls with disabilities.

Figure 1 indicates the key features of gender inequality and disability exclusion, with the nexus indicating where issues for women and girls with disabilities can lead to increased forms of exclusion, as well as new and dynamic barriers and contexts. This nexus is the focus of this set of guidelines. The next section of this publication will address the issues and barriers, as well as opportunities and entry points to address gender inequality. Figure 1 also lists the key priorities in ADB's OP2 for accelerating progress in gender equality in the circle on the right. These priorities will be used throughout these guidelines to identify the ways women and girls with disabilities face increased and different barriers in gaining access to their equal rights to development and how their unique knowledge and skills can be fully utilized in society and contribute to their role as changemakers for a better world.

The approach to addressing the needs of women and girls with disabilities needs to take account of both circles in the figure above:

- Disability inclusion which addresses issues common to all people with disabilities, including issues of accessibility, universal design, reasonable accommodations, assistive technologies and forms of communications, as well as attitudinal, legal, economic, and institutional barriers; and
- Gender equality interventions which address common issues all women experience, such as access to economic resources; decision-making, leadership, policy and legal structures; human development (education, health, and GBV), time poverty and drudgery, and resilience to shocks.

It must also address the specific issues faced exclusively, or at higher or differential rates for women and girls with disabilities. This requires a twin-track approach of addressing the needs of women and girls with disabilities across both disability inclusion and gender equality, as well as including focused and specific actions for women and girls with disabilities. This is identified in the CRPD General Comment 3:

> "States parties must adopt **a twin-track approach** by: (a) systematically mainstreaming the interests and rights of women and girls with disabilities in all national action plans, strategies, and policies concerning women, childhood, and disability, as well as in sectoral plans concerning, for example, gender equality, health, violence, education, political participation, employment, access to justice and social protection; and (b) taking targeted and monitored action aimed specifically at women with disabilities. **A twin-track approach is essential for reducing inequality in respect of participation and the enjoyment of rights.**"[16]

Being able to fully access appropriate and accommodating mainstream services in the disability sector and specific women's services which are disability-inclusive is the ultimate goal for women and girls with disabilities, along with the representation of women with disabilities in all levels of decision-making. However, organizations often focus specifically on either disability inclusion or gender issues, resulting in exclusion of women with disabilities. Women with disabilities can experience sexism and exclusion in the disability sector in both leadership positions and participatory processes as they may be harder to reach or face higher barriers to participation, especially those with sensory, cognitive, and psychosocial disabilities. Additionally, inclusion interventions may not take account of the specific needs of women and girls with disabilities when they face further forms of marginalization, such as faith, ethnicity, caste, class, sexual orientation, or gender identity. It also needs to be noted the women and girls with disabilities face lower employment, poorer levels of health, education, access to social security, decision-making roles, and mobility outside home than that faced by men with disabilities. Likewise, women with disabilities can experience ableism in women's organizations with gender equality initiatives not taking account of the increased stigma and discrimination, rates and forms of GBV, poverty, social isolation of women and girls with disabilities, and the increased care roles and unpaid work of women who are carers for family members with disabilities. This is reflected in the overlapping area in Figure 1 above and aligns with affirmative action for those who are further behind in the development process to ensure they are not "left behind."

A survey conducted by the World Bank in 190 economies assessed the inclusion of gender in disability law and reference to disability in gender legislation. It was found that only 10 economies cross-referenced gender and disability in both pieces of national legislation.[17]

These guidelines aim to identify and address the specific needs of women and girls with disabilities and propose strategies to achieve their transformative empowerment. It does not provide the full analysis of disability exclusion or gender inequality as these are extensively covered by other key ADB resources.

---

[16]   CRPD General comment No. 3 (2016) on women and girls with disabilities, para. 27.
[17]   J. C. Braunmiller and M. Dry. 2022. The Importance of Designing Gender and Disability Inclusive Laws: A Survey of Legislation in 190 Economies. *Global Indicators Briefs* 11. September 12, World Bank, Washington, DC. p. 53.

An example of this approach is addressing gender-responsive and universal design. Universal design is required for all people with disabilities, as is reasonable accommodation, which still may be needed even when universal design is applied due to the diversity of impairments. A gender-responsive approach to universal design is used specifically where women and girls are concerned. For example, safety and security (from sexual harassment and multiple forms of GBV) is an important aspect of gender responsive design. As such, the term gender-responsive universal design is used throughout these guidelines to include some gender modifications that may be needed specifically for women and girls with disabilities, such as including reasonable accommodations in maternal and gynecological equipment, privacy screens, and other modifications.

In addressing disability exclusion, it is also important to recognize the diversity of forms of disability which require different approaches for inclusion. The emerging classification of forms of disability fall into four main categories: physical disabilities; sensory disabilities (predominantly associated with sight and hearing, but also include sensory processing and reduced spatial awareness); cognitive disabilities (which affects intellectual functioning and adaptive behavior of which the common types are autism, attention deficit dyslexia, aphasia, dyscalculia, and memory loss); and psychosocial disabilities (related to mental health which affects social inclusion).[18] Cognitive and psychosocial disabilities are the least addressed forms of impairment in programming for disability inclusion.

Common strategies of disability inclusion for these diverse impairments include universal design (defined earlier in the CRPD), including reasonable accommodations (again defined earlier in the CRPD) which may include communication aids, such as braille, sign language, voice recognition, easy-to -read formats and in local or mother tongue language. In addition, addressing attitudinal, legal, and economic barriers are key strategies of inclusion.[19]

The segregation of gender and disability inclusion is changing, with international, national, and community organizations developing plans, strategies, and working groups that are more inclusive of women and persons with disabilities. There has also been an increase in the creation of women with disabilities groups at all levels. However, these groups are poorly resourced and often rely on women's volunteer labor, reinforcing the unequal, gendered burden of unpaid community work. Making and maintaining contacts with groups of women with disabilities will benefit development programming and aligns with the disability movement motto "nothing about us without us," as well as ADB's approach to developing strategic partnerships with OPDs.

---

[18]   Mental health is defined in a number of ways. The most widely used definition is the one developed by the World Health Organization (WHO), which describes mental health as: "a state of well-being in which an individual realizes his or her own abilities, can cope with the normal stresses of life, can work productively and fruitfully, and is able to make a contribution to his or her community." "Persons with psychosocial disabilities" is the preferred term used by international human rights mechanisms and agencies, as well as by representative organizations of person with disabilities. It encompasses all "persons who, regardless of self-identification or diagnosis of a mental health condition, face restrictions in the exercise of their rights and barriers to participation on the basis of an actual or perceived impairment."

[19]   United Nations. 2020. Sixth session of the Working Group on the Asian and Pacific Decade of Persons with Disabilities, 2013–2022: *Review of recent progress in the implementation of the Asian and Pacific Decade of Persons with Disabilities, 2013–2022: Empowering women and girls with disabilities in Asia and the Pacific.* Bangkok: UN Economic and Social Commission for Asia and the Pacific. para. 19.

Models of Disability

There are several models of disability. The first was a charity or welfare model where disability was seen as a tragedy, with people with disabilities seen as needing to be supported externally by the charitable support of others. This was followed by the medical model which is still widely used as a framework for viewing disability throughout the world. The medical model sees people with disabilities through a deficit model, with their impairment being seen as different from the average "normal" body, thus requiring interventions.

More recently, a social model of disability has been widely accepted by the disability sector which identifies the main problem facing people with disabilities not being their impairments, but how people with various impairments experience the physical and social contexts where they live. These models are summarized in the diagrams below developed by Inclusion London.

The medical and social models of disability[20]

The Medical Model of Disability

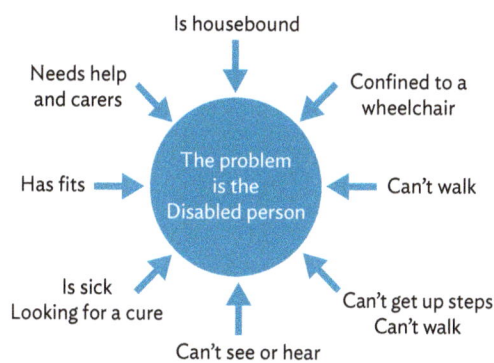

Is housebound

Needs help and carers

Confined to a wheelchair

Has fits

The problem is the Disabled person

Can't walk

Is sick
Looking for a cure

Can't get up steps
Can't walk

Can't see or hear

This is a diagram of the traditional Medical Model of Disability, which the Social Model was developed to challenge.

The Social Model of Disability

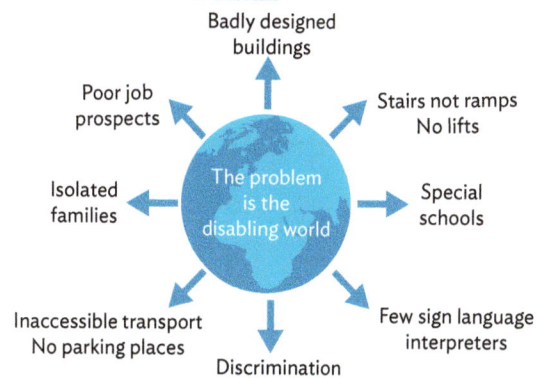

Badly designed buildings

Poor job prospects

Stairs not ramps
No lifts

Isolated families

The problem is the disabling world

Special schools

Inaccessible transport
No parking places

Discrimination

Few sign language interpreters

The Social Model of Disability states that the oppression and exclusion people with impairments face is caused by the way society is run and organised.

Although the medical and social models of disability are the most common frameworks cited, they are not the only ones, and there has been increasing criticism for the social model from various theorists and people with disabilities.

Source: Inclusion London. 2015. *Factsheet: The Social Model of Disability*. London: Inclusion London. pp. 6 and 8. https://www.inclusionlondon.org.uk/wp-content/uploads/2015/05/FactSheets_TheSocialModel.pdf.

Image description: Two diagrams. The first is on the medical model of disability with a set of arrows pointing inward indicating the person with disabilities is the problem. The second diagram is of the social model of disability with arrows pointing outward indicating the problem is the physical and social context of exclusion.

---

20   Inclusion London. 2015. *Factsheet: The Social Model of Disability*. London: Inclusion London. pp. 6 and 8. https://www.inclusionlondon.org.uk/wp-content/uploads/2015/05/FactSheets_TheSocialModel.pdf.

A research report on disability theories and models by the Australian *Royal Commission into violence, abuse, neglect and exploitation of people with disability* has identified cultural and critical theories, including those from feminist disability scholars, and wider intersectionality and disability theorizing from the global south. These approaches are different from the social model in providing a detailed analysis of the hierarchies of power and cognizant of how social norms, beliefs, and practices impact forms of discrimination, exclusion, and violence. Feminist scholars and women with disabilities have critiqued the social model for not addressing the specific cultural gender norms and gendered disability stereotypes and how these impact on women and girls with disabilities, especially related to forms of GBV.[21]

The intersectionality model looks at the connection between sexism and ableism, recognizing how the marginalization of women with disabilities is exacerbated through wider forms of identity such as diversity in age, ethnicity and race, class, caste, among others.[22]

5.2   Using an Intersectionality Approach in Relation to Poverty and to "Leave No One Behind"

The section outlines how different forms of discrimination intersect to exacerbate existing barriers and create new barriers, discrimination, or stigmatization for women and girls with disabilities. Each of these diverse groups deserves additional focus in research due to the current dearth of data and analysis in the sector.

Box 4: Asian Development Bank's Strengthening Disability-Inclusive Development 2021–2025 Road Map

Disability-inclusive development recognizes and is responsive to the intersection of disability with other drivers of discrimination, such as gender, ethnicity, religion, age, and national or social origin, that can compound exclusion and disadvantage.

Source: ADB. 2022. *Strengthening Disability-Inclusive Development 2021–2025 Road Map.* Manila: ADB, p. 4.

---

21   Inclusion London. 2015. *Factsheet: The Social Model of Disability.* London: Inclusion London. p. 21. https://www.inclusionlondon. org.uk/wp-content/uploads/2015/05/FactSheets_TheSocialModel.pdf.

22   Inclusion London. 2015. *Factsheet: The Social Model of Disability.* London: Inclusion London. p. 22. https://www. inclusionlondon.org.uk/wp-content/uploads/2015/05/FactSheets_TheSocialModel.pdf.

5.3   Indigenous Women and Girls with Disabilities

Indigenous peoples experience higher rates of disability, which is identified as a cause and consequence of severe poverty, poorer health, higher levels of violence, and unsafe living conditions.[23] The Indigenous Persons with Disabilities Global Network (IPWDGN) links this to poverty, violence, and greater exposure to environmental degradation and extractive industries, such as mining. In addition, the legacy of colonization has created intergenerational trauma which increases the prevalence of psychosocial disabilities (Figure 2).

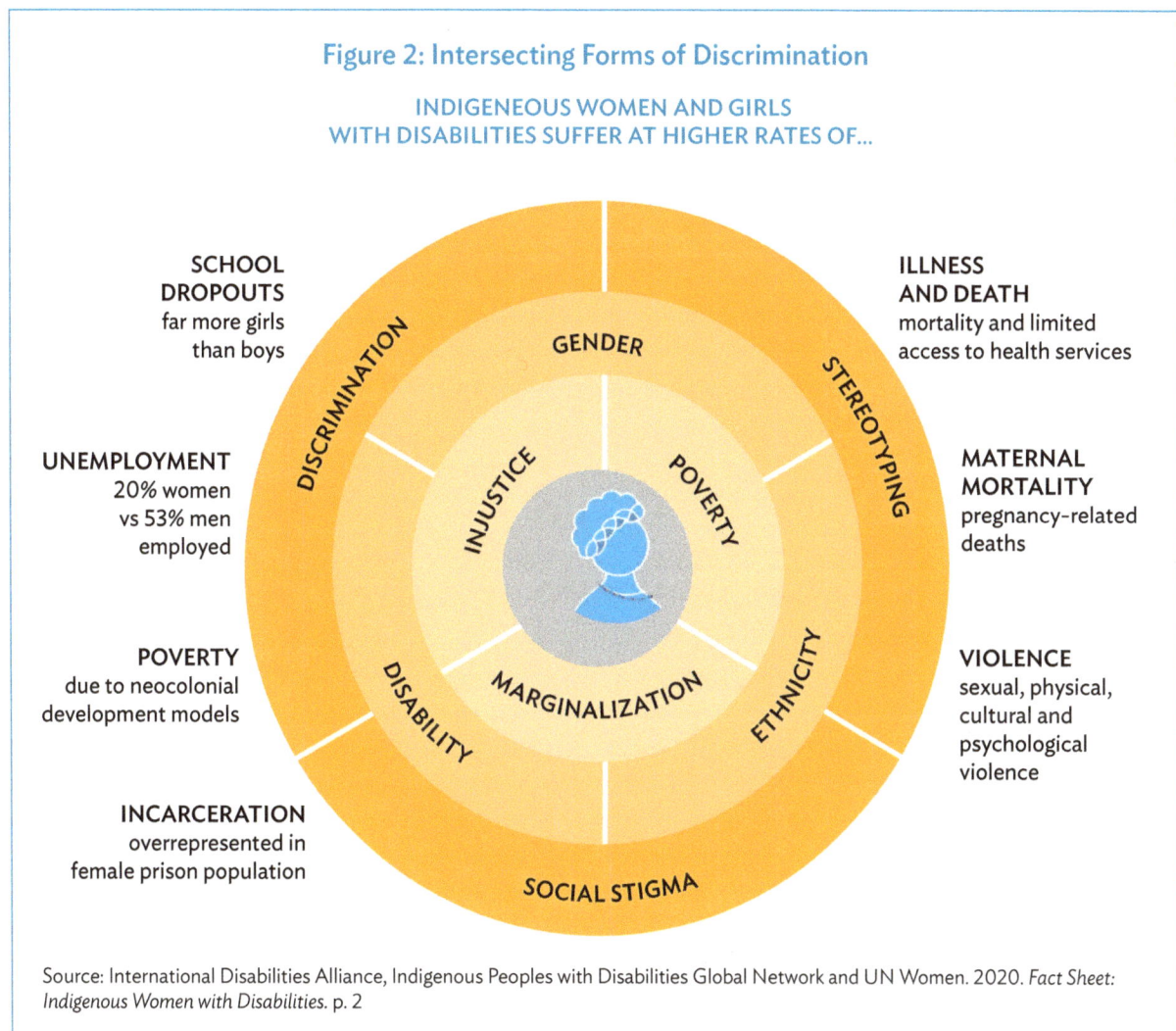

Figure 2: Intersecting Forms of Discrimination

INDIGENEOUS WOMEN AND GIRLS
WITH DISABILITIES SUFFER AT HIGHER RATES OF...

SCHOOL DROPOUTS
far more girls than boys

ILLNESS AND DEATH
mortality and limited access to health services

UNEMPLOYMENT
20% women vs 53% men employed

MATERNAL MORTALITY
pregnancy-related deaths

POVERTY
due to neocolonial development models

VIOLENCE
sexual, physical, cultural and psychological violence

INCARCERATION
overrepresented in female prison population

DISCRIMINATION · GENDER · STEREOTYPING · POVERTY · INJUSTICE · MARGINALIZATION · DISABILITY · ETHNICITY · SOCIAL STIGMA

Source: International Disabilities Alliance, Indigenous Peoples with Disabilities Global Network and UN Women. 2020. *Fact Sheet: Indigenous Women with Disabilities.* p. 2

Image description: A set of concentric circles with personal characteristics and forms of exclusion radiating outward to identify areas where Indigenous women and girls with disabilities face higher rates of social, economic, health and educational disadvantage.

---

23   M. C. Rivas Velarde. 2015. Indigenous persons with disabilities: access to training and employment: discussion paper.Geneva: ILO. p. 2.

These disadvantages combine, interact, and intensify women and girls with disabilities' experience, positioning them at the lowest level of the social hierarchy and often rendering them invisible. IPWDGN suggests this is because society sees Indigenous people with disabilities as "non-contributors" due to disability as well as pervasive stigma related to ethnicity. Diverse impairment is exacerbated by disability-related stigma and stereotyping. This disempowers Indigenous women and girls with disabilities and impacts their ability to claim their rights in the private and public spheres.[24]

As referenced in section 4.3 of this document on international normative frameworks, CEDAW General Recommendation No. 39 (2022) on the *Rights of Indigenous Women and Girls* stresses the high level of discrimination and GBV against Indigenous women and girls with disabilities who are more at risk of living in institutions with risks of systemic violence and forced sterilization due to the denial of their legal capacity.

The National Indigenous Disabled Women Association Nepal (NIDWAN) is focused on addressing this exclusion and has built a network of indigenous women with disabilities across Nepal. After the second World Conference of Indigenous Women in 2021, NIDWAN formed the Indigenous Women with Disabilities Network in Asia to bring together and advocate for Indigenous women with disabilities across Asia.[25]

Box 5: Lived Experience Voices: Indigenous Women with Disabilities

Pratima Gurung is the chair of the National Indigenous Disabled Women Association Nepal, general secretary, Asia focal person of the Indigenous Persons with Disabilities Global Network, and a board member for Women Enabled International.

Pratima acquired her disability at 7 years old when she lost her hand in a truck accident. She stresses the importance of having an intersectional approach during COVID-19 and understanding that Nepalese people can be exposed to multiple sources of discrimination due to their ethnicity, gender, disability, and other characteristics. She stresses that public statements do not include the perspective of indigenous women with disabilities. "Our voices are still unheard," she says. "Information has to represent all persons with disabilities and clearly mentioned, otherwise, we are lumped into one basket and that is how we get excluded, not only during COVID-19, but disaster situations and normal life." Moreover, when presenting government measures and plans, there is no mention of accessibility or gender-specific needs, meaning many groups of the population remain marginalized, due to a lack of an intersectional approach. "Government and development agencies are applying the one-size-fits-all approach," she says. A way of avoiding this is meaningful participation and consultation with different groups to understand that, for instance, the needs of women with disabilities are different than men with disabilities. "This is vital to avoid social exclusion as persons with disabilities are not a homogenous group," says Pratima.

COVID-19 = coronavirus disease.
Source: International Disability Alliance. 2020. *COVID-19 in Nepal: What are the Challenges for Indigenous Persons with Disabilities?* IDA. https://www.internationaldisabilityalliance.org/covid19-indigenous.

---

24   International Disabilities Alliance, Indigenous Peoples with Disabilities Global Network and UN Women. 2020. *Fact Sheet: Indigenous Women with Disabilities.* p. 2 (currently seeking permission for use).
25   Indigenous Persons with Disabilities Global Network (IPWDGN). 2022. Indigenous women with disabilities: a path towards inclusion and collaboration in 2021. https://www.iwgia.org/en/indigenous-persons-with-disabilities-global-network-ipwdgn/4702-iw-2022-ipwdgn.html.

5.4 Discrimination against Girls and Women with Disabilities throughout the Life Cycle

Women and girls with disabilities face discrimination from birth, with girls with congenital disabilities sometimes being killed or left to die. Some girls with disabilities are hidden by their families with little social interaction and are more vulnerable than girls without disabilities (and boys) to physical and mental abuse by family members.[26] Girls with disabilities can also receive less food, with evidence that girls with disabilities may more often be underweight than boys with disabilities and have less access to health care, schooling, and rehabilitation services (see sections on education and health).

Adolescent girls with disabilities continue to face these barriers to education, health, and other services and are at a higher risk of threats to personal safety and security.[27] They are often ignored in sexual and reproductive health (SRH) education and may be subject to forced sterilization and abortion, female genital mutilation, sexual and economic exploitation.[28] (See more on SRH in section 8.1 Health Sector Guidelines.)

Box 6: A Perfect Storm of Exclusion and Marginalization

The Intersection of Disability with Aging, Gender, and Extreme Poverty

Women have longer life expectancy than men and live a greater proportion of their lives in poorer health, resulting in higher rates of disability in older women, heightened by vulnerabilities accumulated across the life course, including lack of access to education, pensions, inheritance, and paid work.

Source: Asian Development Bank. 2022. *Strengthening Disability-Inclusive Development 2021–2025 Road Map*. Manila: ADB. p.9.

In 2020, women made up approximately 62% of the population aged 80 years and over.[29] As many older people do not self-identify as having a disability while still experiencing a physical or mental impairment that substantially limits a major life activity, the prevalence of disability in older women is likely to be underestimated, which has implications for research on the experiences of older women with disabilities.

While women with disabilities experience violence at two to three times the rate of women without disability,[30] older women—especially those with a disability—are rarely addressed in research into violence against women (VAW) (e.g., many surveys on VAW focus on women aged 15–49,

---

[26] UN ESCAP. 1995. *Hidden Sisters: Women and Girls with Disabilities in the Asian and Pacific Region*. Bangkok: ESCAP. p. 1 and 21; N. Groce et al. 2014. Malnutrition and disability: unexplored opportunities for collaboration. *Paediatrics and International Child Health*. p. 312.

[27] PMNCH. 2022. *Global leaders urged to end discriminations that push adolescent girls with disabilities farthest behind in life*. https://pmnch.who.int/news-and-events/news/item/22-03-2022-global-leaders-urged-to-end-discriminations-that-push-adolescent-girls-with-disabilities-farthest-behind-in-life.

[28] CRPD *General comment No. 3. 2016. Women and girls with disabilities*. para. 10.

[29] United Nations Department of Economic and Social Affairs, Population Division. 2020. *World Population Ageing 2020 Highlights: Living arrangements of older persons (ST/ESA/SER.A/451)*. UN.

[30] UN General Assembly. 2012. *Report of the Special Rapporteur on violence against women, its causes and consequences (A/67/227)*. UN.

thus excluding older women). Extensive abuse of women with disabilities has been recorded in nursing homes and institutional settings. WHO estimates one in six people aged 60 and over experienced some form of abuse in community settings during the past year, with two in three staff from nursing homes and long-term care facilities reporting that they have committed abuse in the past year. The physical and psychological impact of this abuse can lead to increased disability for older women.[31]

Lifelong discrimination in the workplace and unequal pay impacts women's economic security, leading older women to have fewer savings and assets and increasing reliance on family members. This is exacerbated for older women with disabilities, with the intersection of gender, age, and disability increasing their vulnerability to abuse, especially economic abuse. CEDAW General Recommendation No. 27: "Older women and protection of their human rights" highlights that older women with disabilities and those living in rural areas receive little to no education, leading to illiteracy and innumeracy that restricts their public, political, and economic participation, and their access to services, entitlements, and recreational activities.[32]

Older women with disabilities rarely hold public decision-making power despite their lived experience and knowledge of their communities. It is essential that policy and programming accounts for the intersecting discriminations faced by older women with disabilities, especially those in poverty, to ensure they are not left behind in the process of development.

Although there is little research on people with diverse SOGIESC with disabilities, a 2020 literature review found that people with diverse SOGIESC with disabilities experience similar issues to other persons with disabilities, as well as increased identity-based stigma, limited access to information and services, and increased, context-specific violence and abuse.[33] There is little reference to people with diverse SOGIESC in many international human rights conventions, let alone people of diverse SOGIESC with disabilities.

Homosexuality was classified as a mental disorder in the *Diagnostic and Statistical Manual of Mental Disorders* from 1952 to 2013, which led to the forced sterilization and institutionalization of people with diverse SOGIESC and persons with disabilities. Stigma and discrimination are still prevalent in many communities which can lead to a fear of accessing health and social services, especially in rural areas (footnote 35).

To address the specific issues faced by people with diverse SOGIESC, it is essential to increase data collection and research, and include the lived experience voices of people with diverse SOGIESC in policy and programming design. Diverse sexualities and gender identities are not legal or are highly discriminated against in many countries. Partnering with OPDs that empower people with diverse SOGIESC, and lesbian, gay, bisexual, trans, intersex, queer, and others (LGBTIQ+) groups that are disability-inclusive, is essential when working in communities to ensure a "do no harm" approach.

[31]   WHO. 2022. *Abuse of older people*. https://www.who.int/news-room/fact-sheets/detail/abuse-of-older-people.

[32]   UN Committee on the Elimination of Discrimination against Women. 2010. *General recommendation No. 27 on older women and protection of their human rights*, 16 December. paras. 16, 19, and 45.

[33]   J. Blyth, K. Alexander, and L. Woolf. 2020. *Out of the Margins: An Intersectional Analysis of Disability and Diverse Sexual Orientation, Gender Identity, Expression and Sex Characteristics in Humanitarian and Development Contexts*. Canberra: DFAT. p.2.

5.5   Other Socially Marginalized Groups

Many women with disabilities experience various other intersecting forms of discrimination and identities that also impact their specific and complex needs and roles in society, including women and girls with disabilities of scheduled caste and scheduled tribe; migrants, refugees, and displaced women and girls with disabilities; those who are illiterate or do not speak the dominant language; single mothers; those that live rural and/or remote areas or within institutions; among others.

Where women and girls with disabilities live can also increase or decrease the risks or opportunities they face. It has been found in some countries that rates of physical and sexual abuse against women and girls with disabilities living in residential facilities was occurring at twice the rate of that for women and girls with disabilities living in the community. Many of these women and girls with disabilities in institutional settings have restricted legal capacity, limiting their right to live independently in the community, their right to informed consent, and their access to reproductive health services (see section 8.1 Health Sector Guidelines).[34] ADB supports the development and implementation of deinstitutionalization policies and programs and expanding the number and scope of independent-living and community-based rehabilitation programs (see *ADB Disability Inclusion Brief*).

The specific forms of intersectional diversity are as broad as the population of women. As such, these guidelines have chosen to use poverty as a crosscutting issue with a specific focus on indigenous or ethnic groups, people of diverse SOGIESC, and women and girls of different ages, while also considering all forms of disability (physical, sensory, psychosocial, and cognitive).

When working with women and girls with disabilities, it is critical to meet with local gender- and disability-inclusive groups and wherever possible, conduct focus group discussions or individual interviews (to respect privacy) with diverse women with disabilities in project sites (Box 7).

Box 7: Lived Experience Voices

"One of the best ways to approach intersectionality is simply to talk to people and ask what they need. However, you have to be proactive and identify what people actually experience. This is how you can learn about intersectionality—but respecting people's privacy is paramount. It is important to create comfortable settings." Key informant, International Disability Alliance.

Source: J. Blyth, K. Alexander, and L. Woolf. 2020. *Out of the Margins: An Intersectional Analysis of Disability and Diverse Sexual Orientation, Gender Identity, Expression and Sex Characteristics in Humanitarian and Development Contexts*. Canberra: DFAT. p.2.

---

[34]   Human Rights Watch. 2020. *Submission to the UN special rapporteur on violence against women, its causes and consequences regarding COVID-19 and the increase of domestic violence against women*. https://www.hrw.org/news/2020/07/03/submission-un-special-rapporteur-violence-against-women-its-causes-and-consequences.

6 Analysis of Needs, Constraints, and Opportunities Faced by Women and Girls with Disabilities

This section highlights the need for a dedicated focus on women and girls with disabilities in line with ADB's OP2 and the targets of SDG5's transformative gender agenda. It sequentially addresses the strategic operational priorities in OP2; however, it does not address the priority on gender equality in human development as the issues of education and health are addressed separately in specific sector guidelines later in this publication. Eliminating violence against women and girls and harmful social norms are also added as a priority area in line with SDG5's gender transformative agenda.

The topics for this section are economic empowerment for women with disabilities; equality for women with disabilities in decision-making and leadership; time poverty and drudgery reduced for women with disabilities and women and girls as carers for family members with disabilities; resilience to external shocks strengthened for diverse women and girls with diverse disabilities; and eliminating harmful social norms and practices and GBV for women and girls with disabilities.

6.1 Economic Empowerment for Women with Disabilities

6.1.1 Key Issues and Barriers

Poverty, lack of education, discrimination, and stigma interact to limit economic opportunities for women with disabilities. Investing in the economic empowerment of women and girls with disabilities is of crucial importance to realize their rights, gender equality, and inclusive economic growth.

- Globally, only 19.6% of women with disabilities are in paid employment, compared to 52.8% of men with disabilities and 29.9% of women without disabilities.[35]
- Only 4% of global businesses are committed to including disability in their strategies.[36]
- Women with disabilities earn on average half the income for similar jobs as men with disabilities.[37]
- Women with disabilities entering the workforce often experience disability-related discrimination, such as perceptions that hiring persons with disabilities reduced productivity (footnote 39).
- Women with disabilities are perceived as powerless, lacking in value (footnote 39) or leadership and entrepreneurial capacity (footnote 39).

---

[35] CBM. 2016. *Inclusion Counts: The Economic Case for Disability-Inclusive Development.* Bensheim, Germany: CBM. p. 71.
[36] UN. 2020. *Sixth session of the Working Group on the Asian and Pacific Decade of Persons with Disabilities, 2013–2022: Review of recent progress in the implementation of the Asian and Pacific Decade of Persons with Disabilities, 2013–2022.* Bangkok: UN Economic and Social Commission for Asia and the Pacific.
[37] ILO. 2018. *Care Work and Care Jobs for the Future of Decent Work.* Geneva: ILO. p. 165.

Figure 3: Key Issues and Barriers to Economic Empowerment for Women with Disabilities

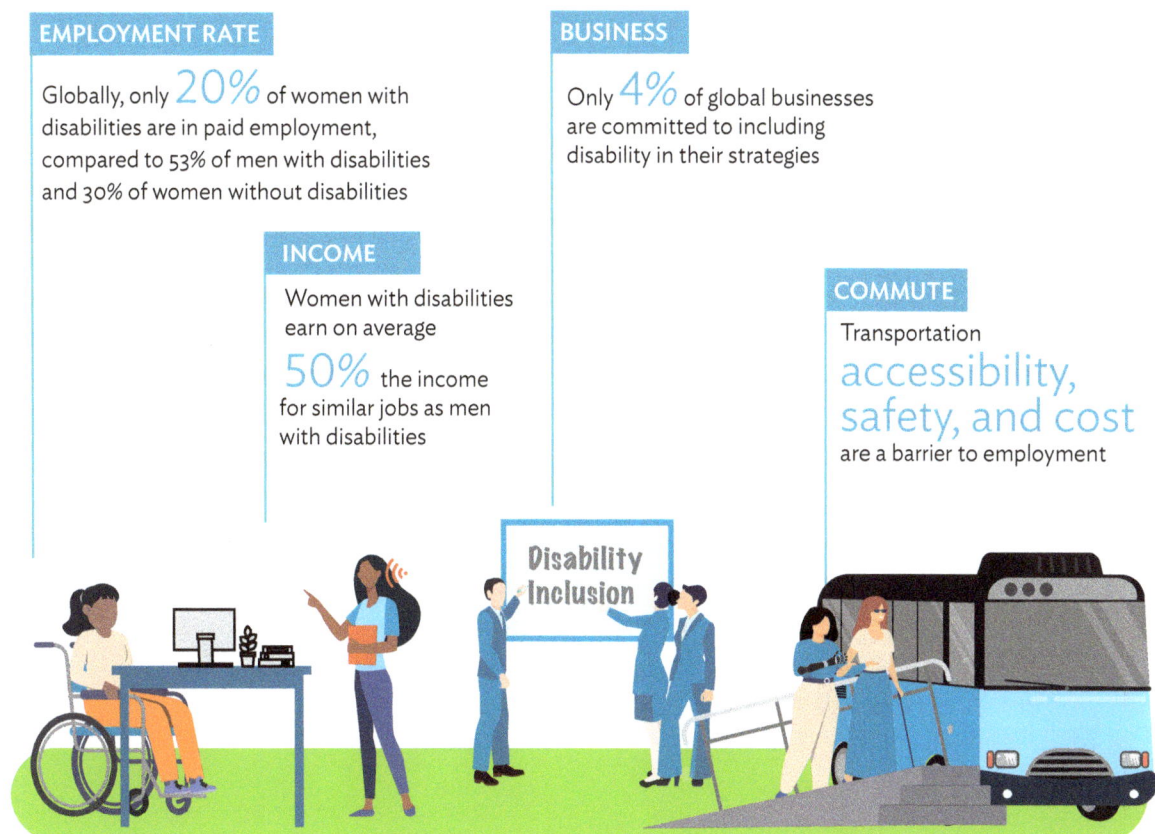

EMPLOYMENT RATE

Globally, only 20% of women with disabilities are in paid employment, compared to 53% of men with disabilities and 30% of women without disabilities

BUSINESS

Only 4% of global businesses are committed to including disability in their strategies

INCOME

Women with disabilities earn on average 50% the income for similar jobs as men with disabilities

COMMUTE

Transportation accessibility, safety, and cost are a barrier to employment

Disability Inclusion

Sources: CBM. 2016. *Inclusion Counts: The Economic Case for Disability-Inclusive Development.* Bensheim, Germany: CBM. p. 71. UN. 2020. *Sixth session of the Working Group on the Asian and Pacific Decade of Persons with Disabilities, 2013–2022: Review of recent progress in the implementation of the Asian and Pacific Decade of Persons with Disabilities, 2013–2022.* Bangkok: UN Economic and Social Commission for Asia and the Pacific. ILO. 2018. *Care Work and Care Jobs for the Future of Decent Work.* Geneva: ILO. p. 165.

- In a World Bank study of legislation in 190 economies, it was identified that although 111 economies included reasonable accommodations in laws and policies, only six of these directly mentioned women with disabilities. Similarly, of 120 economies where employment laws and policies specifically addressed incentives for people for disabilities, only five specifically referenced women with disabilities.[38]
- Women with disabilities perform unpaid care in families, reducing opportunities for full-time paid employment.
- Women with disabilities in paid employment tend to work longer hours, receive lower wages, lack job security, and have fewer opportunities for promotion than men with disabilities or women without disabilities (footnote 40).
- Paid employment in the care sector is poorly paid and has a low status (footnote 40).

---

[38]   World Bank. 2023. *Including Women and Girls with Disabilities in World Bank Operations: Toolkit.* Washington, DC: World Bank. p. 56.

(a) Paid care work is direct care for persons performed within a household or institution for pay or profit. Paid care work spans both public and private spheres and is provided in a variety of settings, in both formal and informal economies. Care work is a significant source of work for women globally (footnote 40).

(b) A paid care worker looks after the physical, psychological, emotional, and developmental needs of others within an employment relationship. Care occupations are inaccurately viewed as unskilled or as an extension of women's role as caregivers. This stereotype contributes to women's low status, low pay, and lack of recognition in the work they do (footnote 40).

- Many working women with disabilities are self-employed with limited support available for care, assistance with household roles, or access to accommodations or rehabilitation.

- Limited education and poor literacy reduce women with disabilities access to, or awareness of, workplace policies, procedures, rights, and entitlements.

- Women with disabilities may be reluctant to disclose their disability type or limitation, for fear of losing their employment. Lower levels of education, literacy, and numeracy at all levels limit women with disabilities' work opportunities and reduce participation and benefit from training schemes.

- Workplace barriers to access and participation in the workplace include
   (a) gendered disability discrimination,
   (b) lack of approaches tailored to the specific needs of women,
   (c) tokenistic approaches to addressing functional impairments, and
   (d) lack of diversity and inclusion policies and practices.

- Transportation accessibility, safety, and cost are a barrier to employment (footnote 40).

6.1.2 Opportunities and Entry Points

Figure 4: Opportunities to Promote Employment and Retention for Women with Disabilities

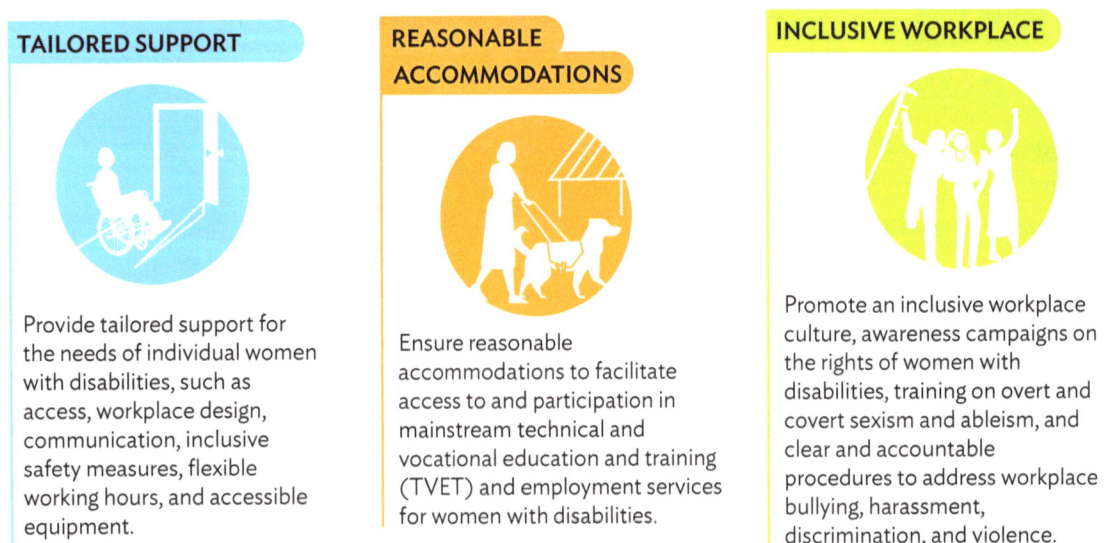

TAILORED SUPPORT

Provide tailored support for the needs of individual women with disabilities, such as access, workplace design, communication, inclusive safety measures, flexible working hours, and accessible equipment.

REASONABLE ACCOMMODATIONS

Ensure reasonable accommodations to facilitate access to and participation in mainstream technical and vocational education and training (TVET) and employment services for women with disabilities.

INCLUSIVE WORKPLACE

Promote an inclusive workplace culture, awareness campaigns on the rights of women with disabilities, training on overt and covert sexism and ableism, and clear and accountable procedures to address workplace bullying, harassment, discrimination, and violence.

Source: Author.

- Adopting inclusive recruitment policies. Women with disabilities, especially those who are household heads, as well as women who are caregivers for their parents or their children with disabilities require reasonable accommodations in the workplace.
- Providing specific training and skill development opportunities relevant for diverse women with disabilities within their local communities (see case study 7.2.4: Vocational training the Lao People's Democratic Republic [the Lao PDR] which trains women with disabilities in sign language).
- Clearly articulating employment pathways and progression within an organization, including mentoring and/or coaching.[39]

Box 8: Lived Experience Voices: Economic Empowerment for Women with Disabilities in Timor-Leste

Magdalena Soares is a woman with a disability in Timor-Leste. She never went to school and taught herself to read and write. She says, "people stare at me often because of my physical impairment, but my disability does not stop me from living independently and successfully."

Through her involvement in the Government of Australia's Partnership for Human Development (PHD) implemented through Abt Associates Australia, Magdalena has built her skills, technical knowledge, and confidence and is now employed as an administration officer for Ra'es Hadomi Timor Oan (RHTO). She is also the founder of the first Disabled People's Organization (DPO) for women with disabilities in Timor-Leste.

Image description: Magdalena Soares walking toward building wearing a face mask. (photo care of PHD program).

The PHD incorporates gender equality and disability inclusion into their work across health, education, and social protection sectors to increase health, nutrition, and literacy outcomes. The program supports DPOs in Timor-Leste to help women with disabilities overcome barriers to economic opportunities. The program mandates 50% of the RHTO's field officer positions are held by women with disabilities and provides training and mentoring to build technical knowledge. For many of these women, it is their first-ever paid position and several have progressed their careers. Adopting a strengths-based approach and drawing on their lived experience in overcoming barriers, women in the program have become role models for other women with disabilities.

Strengthening DPOs in Timor-Leste has enabled these organizations to advocate for inclusive and accountable government policies. This had led to the establishment of the National Directorate for Promotion and Protection of the Rights for People with Disability and the development of the National Disability Action Plan which provide annual planning and budgeting to deliver more inclusive services.

Source: D. N. Fátima da Cunha and R. Devitt. 2022. What does "inclusive growth" mean for women with disabilities? DFAT. hcesttps://abtgovernance.com/2022/03/08/what-does-inclusive-growth-mean-for-women-with-disabilities/.

---

[39] ILO. 1983. *Vocational Rehabilitation and Employment Convention (No. 159): Principles of Vocational Rehabilitation and Employment Policies for Disabled Persons.* Geneva: ILO.

The 2018 UN *Disability and Development Report* advocates special measures, such as gender targets that oblige employers to hire a percentage of persons with disabilities, typically ranging from 1% to 15%. It suggests the most effective quota systems include a payment levy for every position not held by people with disabilities for noncompliant companies. These levies can form a special fund to support initiatives for persons with disabilities. As such, DMCs can promote gender targets by:

(i)   Prohibiting discrimination on the grounds of disability.
(ii)   Setting targets for inclusive employment practices ensuring a gendered lens.
(iii) Developing policy and providing incentives to employers that meet and maintain a percentage of people with disabilities in their workforce and/or implementing quotas and payment levies for noncompliance.
(iv)   Utilizing revenue raised from noncompliance quota levies be used to conduct awareness campaigns and promote persons with disabilities into employment, particularly opportunities for women and girls with disabilities to overcome barriers and exclusions to their education, training, and employment opportunity.
(v)   Providing financial support to access mainstream technical and vocational education and training.
(vi)   Ensuring entrepreneurship and microfinance programs and initiatives include persons with disabilities.
(vii) Ensuring employment policies, including return to work and retention of positions, facilitate the needs of persons with disabilities.[40]

6.2 Equality for Women with Disabilities in Decision-Making and Leadership

6.2.1 Key Issues and Barriers

There are significant gaps and limitations in the global data on women with disabilities in leadership positions.[41] Additionally, quality data is essential to track the advancement of women throughout formal decision-making processes.

- In a study of 18 economies in the Asia and Pacific region in 2017, it was found that only four economies had a woman with disabilities in national legislative bodies. Within these four economies, the share of women parliamentarians with disabilities ranged from 0.3% to 6.3%.[42]

- A 2021 global study conducted by Women, Business and the Law (WBL) assessing the rights of women with disabilities in 190 economies, found that while the number of economies with disability laws increased almost threefold within 1990–2022, only about one-third of them specifically address women.[43]

[40] UN. 2018. *Disability and Development Report: Realizing the Sustainable Development. Goals by, for and with Persons with Disabilities.* UN Department of Economic and Social Affairs. p. 10.
[41] UN. 2018. *Disability and Development Report: Realizing the Sustainable Development.*
[42] UN Women. n.d. *Facts and figures: Women and girls with disabilities: Leadership and political participation.* https://www.unwomen. org/en/what-we-do/women-and-girls-with-disabilities/facts-and-figures.
[43] World Bank. 2022. *Global Indicators Briefs No. 11: The Importance of Designing Gender and Disability Inclusive Laws: A Survey of Legislation in 190 Economies.* p. 5.

Figure 5: Women with Disabilities Are Severely Underrepresented in Decision-Making

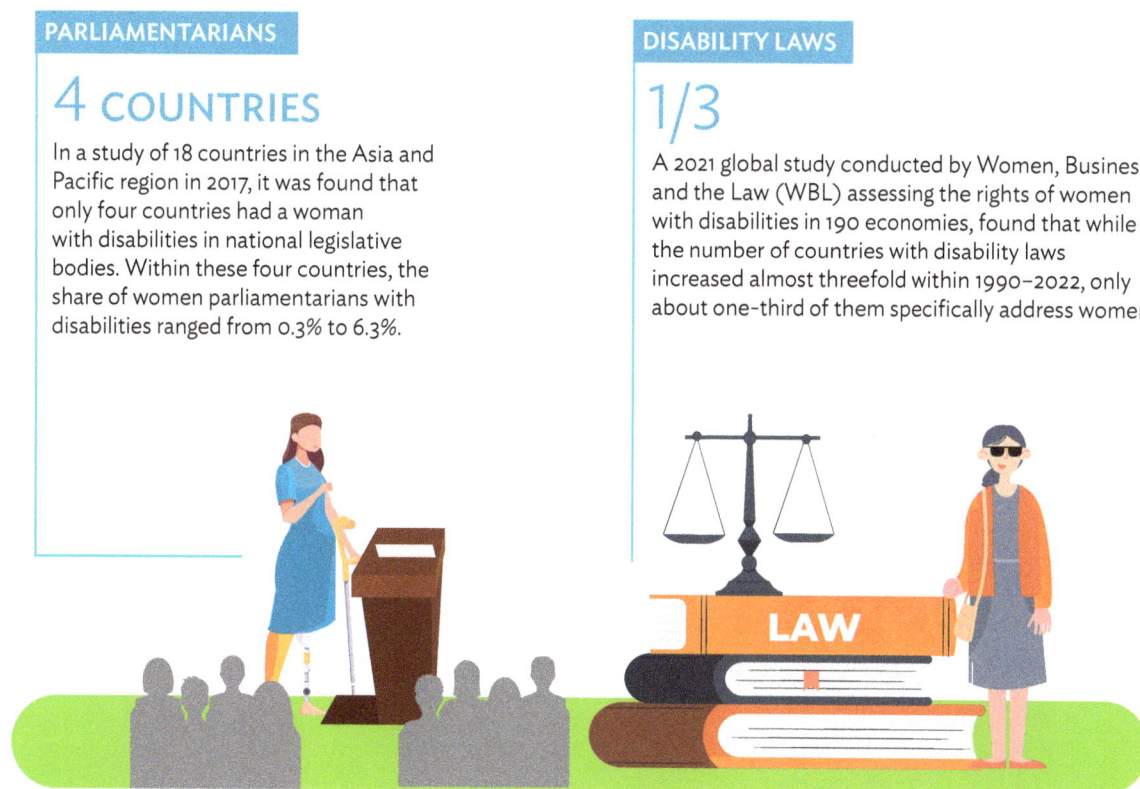

PARLIAMENTARIANS

4 COUNTRIES

In a study of 18 countries in the Asia and Pacific region in 2017, it was found that only four countries had a woman with disabilities in national legislative bodies. Within these four countries, the share of women parliamentarians with disabilities ranged from 0.3% to 6.3%.

DISABILITY LAWS

1/3

A 2021 global study conducted by Women, Business and the Law (WBL) assessing the rights of women with disabilities in 190 economies, found that while the number of countries with disability laws increased almost threefold within 1990–2022, only about one-third of them specifically address women.

Sources: UN Women. n.d. *Facts and figures: Women and girls with disabilities: Leadership and political participation.* https://www.unwomen.org/en/what-we-do/women-and-girls-with-disabilities/facts-and-figures. World Bank. 2022. *Global Indicators Briefs No. 11: The Importance of Designing Gender and Disability Inclusive Laws: A Survey of Legislation in 190 Economies.* p. 5.

- Women with disabilities' decision-making roles throughout the community are limited due to lower levels of education, discrimination, and stigma. Their public participation is also limited due to barriers in accessing transport and harassment on transport, which can lead to isolation. They are often unable to go out and engage in active community life even if they wish to due to social norms and stigma. This can be more acute for persons with sensory impairments, as transport infrastructure may be inaccessible.[44]

Women with disabilities are often denied their right to legal capacity and face barriers to accessing justice:

- The CRPD General Comment 3 refers to "their rights to maintain control over their reproductive health, including on the basis of free and informed consent, to found a family, to choose where and with whom to live, to physical and mental integrity, to own and inherit property, to control their own financial affairs and to have equal access to bank loans, mortgages, and other forms of financial credit are often violated through patriarchal systems of substituted decision-making."[45]

---

[44] UN Women. 2022. *Assessment of the needs of women and girls with disabilities and the state of protection of their rights in Georgia.* Tbilisi: UN Women. p. 33.

[45] CRPD General Comment 3. para 51.

- General Comment 3 also refers to harmful stereotypes, discrimination, and lack of access to reasonable accommodations can result in a lack of perceived credibility and their claims in the justice system may be dismissed.[46]
- Forced sterilization can be ordered by a judge, a parent, or a legal guardian.[47]
- Women with disabilities are underrepresented in national coordination mechanisms on disability matters.
- In 2017, across 17 economies or areas in the Asia and Pacific region, DPOs included nearly twice as many men as women, representing 21% (for men) and 12% (for women) of all mechanisms. Men were similarly overrepresented in other types of organizations, making up 43% of all mechanism members, compared to 24% for women. In seven of those same 17 countries, national machineries for gender equality included no women with disabilities among their membership. In the remaining five countries, only 9% of members were women with disabilities (footnote 49).
- The CRPD states that due to power imbalances and multiple forms of discrimination, they have fewer opportunities to establish or join organizations that can represent their needs as women, children, and persons with disabilities.[48]

6.2.2 Opportunities and Entry Points

Entry points addressing gender equality in decision-making and leadership and the regulatory, legal, and institutional environment for gender equality should be specifically aligned to the commitments made by the CRPD and implementation of the Incheon Strategy.

- The CRPD General Comment 3 calls for national governments support and promote "the creation of organizations and networks of women with disabilities and supporting and encouraging women with disabilities to take leadership roles in public decision-making bodies at all levels."[49]
- In a report to the Human Rights Council in January 2016, the *Report of the Special Rapporteur on the rights of persons with disabilities* states that "countries must take steps to eliminate the barriers that prevent their [women's] participation in public decision-making and must ensure that all participatory mechanisms and bodies take into account both disability- and gender-related factors and the complex interrelationships between them."[50] It also states that "countries should reach out directly to women and girls with disabilities, especially when cultural and social backgrounds make it unsafe for them to participate in open consultations. States must also establish adequate measures to guarantee that the perspectives of women and girls with disabilities are fully taken into account and that they will not suffer any reprisals for expressing their viewpoints and concerns, especially in relation to sexual and reproductive rights, gender-based violence and sexual violence."[51]

---

[46] UN. 2016. *CRPD General Comment No. 3 (2016) Women and Girls with disabilities: Situations of risk and humanitarian emergencies (art. 11)*. Geneva: UN. Article 52.

[47] World Bank. 2022. *Global Indicators Briefs No. 11: The Importance of Designing Gender and Disability Inclusive Laws: A Survey of Legislation in 190 Economies*. Washington, DC: World Bank Group.

[48] World Bank. 2022. *Global Indicators Briefs No. 11: The Importance of Designing Gender and Disability Inclusive Laws: A Survey of Legislation in 190 Economies*. Washington, DC: World Bank Group. Article 60.

[49] UN. 2016. *CRPD General Comment No. 3*. para. 64 (d).

[50] OHCHR. 2016. *A/HRC/31/62 Report of the Special Rapporteur on the rights of persons with disabilities to participate in decision-making*. Geneva: OHCHR. para. 58.

[51] OHCHR. 2016. *A/HRC/31/62 Report of the Special Rapporteur on the rights of persons with disabilities to participate in decision-making*. Geneva: OHCHR. para. 59.

- General Comment 3 also states national governments should repeal any law or policy that prevents women with disabilities from effectively and fully participating in political and public life on an equal basis with others, including in respect of the right to form and join organizations and networks of women, in general, and of women with disabilities, in particular.[52][53]

Figure 6: Entry Points for Governments to Ensure a Focus on Women with Disabilities in National Gender Policies and Decision-Making Bodies

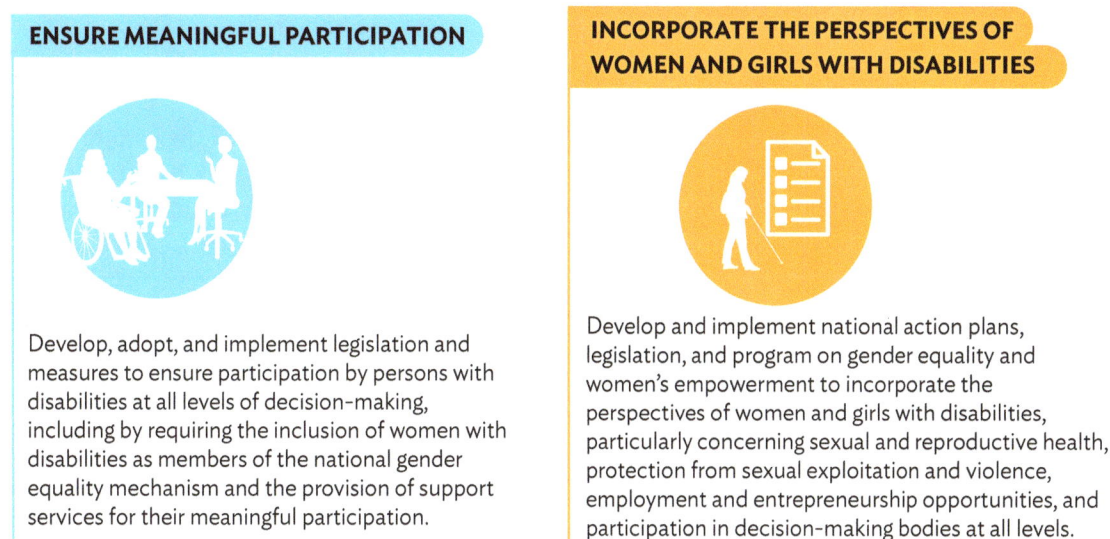

ENSURE MEANINGFUL PARTICIPATION

Develop, adopt, and implement legislation and measures to ensure participation by persons with disabilities at all levels of decision-making, including by requiring the inclusion of women with disabilities as members of the national gender equality mechanism and the provision of support services for their meaningful participation.

INCORPORATE THE PERSPECTIVES OF WOMEN AND GIRLS WITH DISABILITIES

Develop and implement national action plans, legislation, and program on gender equality and women's empowerment to incorporate the perspectives of women and girls with disabilities, particularly concerning sexual and reproductive health, protection from sexual exploitation and violence, employment and entrepreneurship opportunities, and participation in decision-making bodies at all levels.

Source: Author.

6.3 Time Poverty and Drudgery Reduced for Women with Disabilities and Women and Girls as Carers for Family Members with Disabilities

6.3.1 Key Issues and Barriers

The work performed in both the unpaid and paid care sector is dominated by women:

- An unpaid carer is a person who provides unpaid care or support to individuals within their household or community, including persons with disabilities.
- Women perform the majority of unpaid care work and represent the majority of unpaid carers around the world, performing over 75% of all unpaid care work globally.[54]
- Women and girls are disproportionately responsible for unpaid care and domestic work: globally women and girls spend three times as much time on this work as men and boys (footnote 57).

---

[52]   UN. 2016. *CRPD General Comment No. 3.* para. 64 (a).
[53]   UN. 2018. Action Plan to accelerate the implementation of the Incheon Strategy, Actions 11 b. and 15 a.
[54]   ILO. 2018. *Care Work and Care Jobs for the Future of Decent Work.* Geneva: ILO.

- Unpaid care work is one of the main barriers preventing women from moving into paid employment and better-quality jobs (footnote 57).

Unpaid care work provides no income to women, who are primary carers of family members with disabilities. Gross domestic product calculations do not include preparation of meals, laundry, cleaning, shopping, care of children, older people, the sick and persons with disabilities, and volunteer services provided through organizations and groups.[55]

Carers of children with disabilities (CWD) report feeling overwhelmed due to lack of knowledge of the types of disability and particular care needed. Carers lack knowledge on the following:[56]

- Children with disabilities have particular developmental requirements.
- What constitutes quality of care, and the importance of providing quality care as defined by United Nations Children's Fund (UNICEF) as the right type of care for one's health condition; care that results in the best possible outcome; care delivered with attention to one's concerns, needs, and life goals; and care that keeps one safe from hazards and harm.[57]

Women with disabilities are often assumed to be unproductive and noncontributors to the home and society; however, they conduct extensive unpaid work, as identified in the UN 2018 *Disability and Development Report*:[58]

- Data limitations mean the role of women with disabilities in the unpaid care sector is less known.
- Data collected by United Nations Department of Economic and Social Affairs (UN DESA) of eight developing countries found that women with disabilities were more likely to be engaged in unpaid work than women without disabilities in all but one country (Indonesia).
- Women with disabilities are often limited to unpaid work roles, especially within the household. This stems from difficulties in accessing paid employment.

6.3.2   Opportunities and Entry Points

- Article 19 in the CRPD and CPRD General Comment 5 address independent living and personal assistance. Persons with disabilities have a right to choose who helps them with daily care tasks, as well as other daily living activities. Promoting the right to choose their own form of personal assistance can promote the rights of women in the household not to be the default carer.
- Promote allowances and other employment rights (e.g., pension contributions, social insurance, social service schemes for carers) for personal assistants to help ensure that women who provide personal assistance or daily care (through empowered negotiation with the persons with disabilities in the household) are paid and their work is recognized as labor with all the commensurate labor rights.

---

[55]   ADB. 2020. *Women's Time Use in Rural Tajikistan*. Manila: ADB.
[56]   Department of Social Welfare of the Ministry of Gender, Children and Social Protection and UNICEF Ghana. 2020. *Training Manual for Caregivers of Children with Disabilities*. Accra: UNICEF.
[57]   Department of Social Welfare of the Ministry of Gender, Children and Social Protection and UNICEF Ghana. 2020. *Training Manual for Caregivers of Children with Disabilities*. Accra: UNICEF. p. 74.
[58]   UN. 2018. *Disability and Development Report: Realizing the Sustainable Development Goals by, for and with persons with disabilities*. UN Department of Economic and Social Affairs. p. 109.

Figure 7: Entry Points to Reduce Time Poverty and Drudgery for Women with Disabilities and Women and Girls as Carers for Family Members with Disabilities

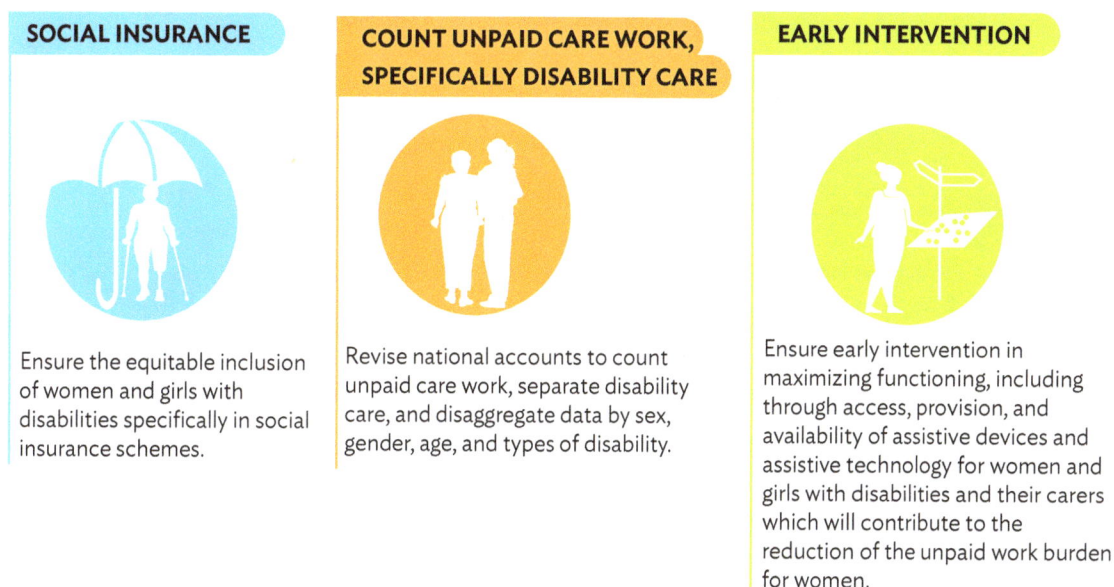

SOCIAL INSURANCE

Ensure the equitable inclusion of women and girls with disabilities specifically in social insurance schemes.

COUNT UNPAID CARE WORK, SPECIFICALLY DISABILITY CARE

Revise national accounts to count unpaid care work, separate disability care, and disaggregate data by sex, gender, age, and types of disability.

EARLY INTERVENTION

Ensure early intervention in maximizing functioning, including through access, provision, and availability of assistive devices and assistive technology for women and girls with disabilities and their carers which will contribute to the reduction of the unpaid work burden for women.

Source: Author.

- Provide flexible working conditions in the formal sector for women who are carers of family members with disabilities.
- Provide capacity building for parents (especially mothers) in strategies to assist children and family members with disabilities, especially in areas of cognitive and psychosocial disabilities.
- Provide psychological and social support networks and respite opportunities for mothers and other family members who are the primary carers for family members with disabilities.
- Increase skills of local health and education services to equip them to identify disabilities and provide disability support to address the needs of all types of disability in the community.

6.4 Resilience to External Shocks Strengthened for Diverse Women and Girls with Diverse Disabilities

6.4.1 Key Issues and Barriers

For over 2 decades, there has been a significant focus on the needs and concerns of women in humanitarian crises which was recognized in the UN Security Council Resolution 1325 on women, peace, and security. However, this resolution does not address disability. Likewise, while there has been significant work done on addressing the needs of women in disaster risk reduction, disability inclusion is rarely implemented. Approaches to social inclusion are broadening; however, addressing the specific issues faced by women and girls with disabilities in development processes are rarely identified. An exception to this is the COVID-19 pandemic where persons with disabilities have been a focus of study and intervention due to higher risks with preexisting health issues. The escalated risks for women and girls with disabilities, and the absence of their voices in national health planning has led to global and national advocacy, with several guidance notes and resources focusing on women and girls with disabilities. Barriers and unique threats to women and girls with disabilities resilience are outlined below, followed by recommendations for entry points to build their resilience, acknowledge their capabilities, and highlight the importance of their voices in being agents for change.

Figure 8: Key Issues and Barriers to Women and Girls with Disabilities'
Resilience to External Shocks

RESILIENCE TO EXTERNAL SHOCKS

Women and girls with disabilities are disproportionately affected by crises, including climate-related extreme weather events, humanitarian crises, and the COVID-19 pandemic.

LACK OF DISABILITY-DISAGGREGATED DATA

Governments and relief agencies may lack information on how many women and girls with disabilities are or will be affected by diverse crises.

TARGETED POLICIES

The lack of gender, age, ethnicity, geography, and disability disaggregated data makes it difficult to carry out evidence-based analysis of the socioeconomic impact of crises and to facilitate targeted and mainstreamed policies for women and girls with disabilities.

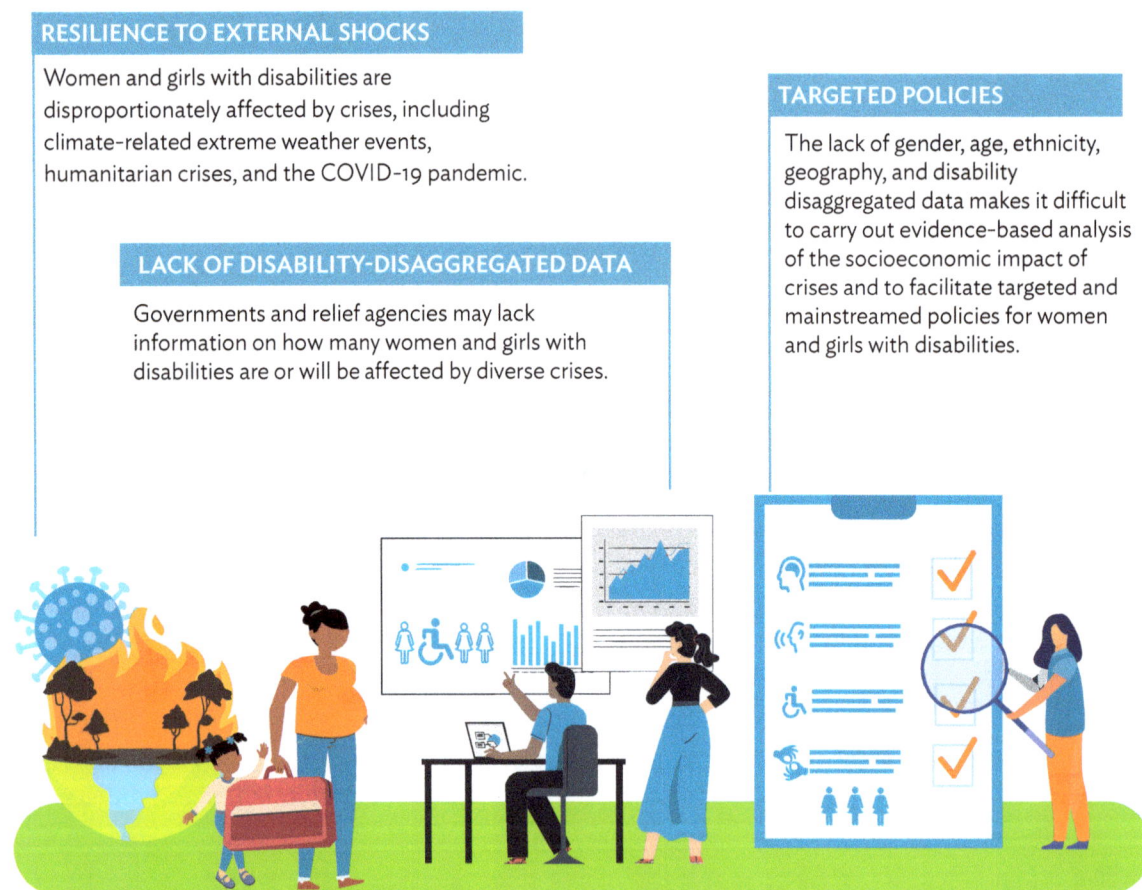

COVID-19 = coronavirus disease.
Source: Pacific Women Shaping Pacific Development. 2021. *Thematic Brief: Inclusion of Pacific Women with Disabilities.* Canberra: Australian Aid. p. 1. Women Enabled International. 2017. *Comments on Draft CEDAW General Recommendation on Gender Related Dimensions of Disaster Risk Reduction in a Changing Climate.* Geneva: OHCHR.

Women and girls with disabilities are disproportionately affected by crises, including climate-related extreme weather events, humanitarian crises, and the COVID-19 pandemic.[59]

---

[59]   Pacific Women Shaping Pacific Development. 2021. *Thematic Brief: Inclusion of Pacific Women with Disabilities.* Canberra: Australian Aid. p. 1.

Governments and relief agencies may lack information on how many women and girls with disabilities are or will be affected by diverse crises. Although women and children are seen as a priority for relief distribution, focused preparedness planning has not been systemically integrated into systems for delivering relief services for women and girls with disabilities. This should address universal design for infrastructure, reasonable accommodations, and appropriate forms of communication targeting women and girls with disabilities, especially those living in poverty.[60]

The lack of gender, age, ethnicity, geography, and disability disaggregated data makes it difficult to carry out evidence-based analysis of the socioeconomic impact of crises and to facilitate targeted and mainstreamed policies for women and girls with disabilities.

Women with disabilities remain responsible for caregiving during crises, impacting their ability to address their own needs. Single women with disabilities with children or single mothers with children with disabilities may lack access to family, friends, or caregivers during crises. This disproportionately affects internally displaced women who lack family support structures.

Gender, disability, structural and historical inequalities have been exacerbated by the multifaceted impact of the COVID-19 crisis. This includes limitations to accessing carers and home support and escalated stigma for those requiring additional care in the health care system.[61] For poor women with disabilities, the affordability of health care and lack of or limited health insurance and other forms of social protection limit specific assistance targeted to women and girls with disabilities.

> "Developing robust early warning systems that are responsive to gender, age, and disability is a crucial way to ensure equitable access to information before a crisis occurs."[62]

Women and girls with disabilities face various barriers to accessing response and recovery assistance:

- The ability of women and girls with disabilities to flee disasters may be compromised due to physical barriers and inaccessibility of early warning information. Additionally, family and community members may be unable or unwilling to transport women with disabilities following a disaster, prioritizing children and other family members, leaving them abandoned in their homes.

- Disaster and humanitarian services, including food, clothing, shelter, and financial assistance are more likely to be inaccessible to women with disabilities due to lack of accommodations in communications combined with less assertiveness due their limited self-advocacy skills. Similarly, women with disabilities also face disparities in accessing health services, including sexual and reproductive health information and services following disasters and crises (see section 8.1 Health Sector Guidelines).

---

60 Women Enabled International. 2017. *Comments on Draft CEDAW General Recommendation on Gender Related Dimensions of Disaster Risk Reduction in a Changing Climate.* Geneva: OHCHR.

61 United Nations Department of Economic and Social Affairs. 2020. *Leaving no one behind: The COVID-19 crisis through the disability and gender lens.* New York: UN DESA. p. 1.

62 Women Enabled International. 2017. *Comments on Draft CEDAW General Recommendation on Gender Related Dimensions of Disaster Risk Reduction in a Changing Climate.* Geneva: OHCHR.

- Women with disabilities often experience difficulty in accessing emergency assistance relief information as this is generally targeted to men. Additionally, information is often not available in accessible formats or appropriate for their needs, such as helplines and hotlines and/or when they do receive information, they may not be able to physically access distribution points or communicate with staff.[63]

- Female refugees, migrants, and asylum seekers with disabilities may be denied access to formal and nonformal education, as well as rights to access health and justice systems if they do not have citizenship or residence status (footnote 66).

Box 9: Impacts of Climate Change on Indigenous Women with Disabilities

National Indigenous Disabled Women's Organization Nepal (NIDWAN) conducted a rapid qualitative assessment on the Impacts of Climate Change on Indigenous Women with Disabilities in Ward 2 Namobuddha Municipality, Nepal. The research aimed to document evidence on the impacts of climate change on indigenous women with disabilities. The results illustrated the differential and extensive impact of climate change on Indigenous women with disabilities in regard to gender equality and social exclusion through historically discriminatory social structures, situational vulnerability, and compounded intersectional impacts based on indigeneity, gender, and disability.[a]

The majority of Indigenous peoples in Nepal (including women with disabilities) are farmers and are still dependent on forests for their livelihoods. They have a symbiotic relationship with the forest and natural resources. The sustainable management of forests and biodiversity is integral to their distinct identity and customary practices, and a practice they pass on to future generations.[b]

The role of women, Indigenous women, and Indigenous women with disabilities as actors and agents of change is crucial. Indigenous women and women with disabilities have critical knowledge and proposals to contribute to discussions on confronting the climate crisis, but they are excluded from these decision-making spaces. Women with disabilities are not just victims, but we are key to solutions, which needs to be realized in climate policies and plans with concrete implementation. Stakeholders such as states, United Nations agencies, development partners, and community service organizations working on climate justice must listen to the voices of social groups with multiple identities like indigenous women and indigenous women with disabilities, who know how to fight and stand up for their rights. These stakeholders should encourage ambitious women who will not lose sight of what is important (note b).

[a] NIDWAN. 2021. Impacts of Climate Change on Indigenous Women with Disabilities. https://nidwan.org.np/2021/10/03/research-on-impacts-of-climate-change-on-indigenous-women-with-disabilities/.

[b] P. Gurung, 2021. Indigenous women with disabilities are not just victims but we are key to climate solutions. Global Alliance for Green and Gender Action. https://gaggaalliance.org/indigenous-women-with-disabilities-are-not-just-victims-but-we-are-key-to-climate-solutions/?fbclid=IwAR2IgStHnSdPC5o9N-m_oCCJkQiR7bq9xEoseFQ0uCTIBMGWvSfDmxJqHNY.

---

[63] UN. 2016. *CRPD General Comment No. 3 (2016) Women and Girls with disabilities: Situations of risk and humanitarian emergencies (art. 11)*. Geneva: UN.

Women with disabilities are at a higher risk of GBV and sexual exploitation in times of crisis:[64]

- Women with disabilities report higher incidence of GBV during crises. Overcrowded and poorly lit shelters or refugee camps may lack accessible toilets and washing facilities, heightening the risk of experiencing violence.

- Refugee camps can be unsafe places for children with disabilities, especially girls. Gender- and disability-responsive child protection measures are generally not enforced.[65]

- Women with disabilities are less likely to have access to justice and post-conflict reconciliation activities where specific accessible or inclusive processes are not highlighted.[66]

Indigenous women and girls with disabilities are further exposed to crisis and emergency contexts. Indigenous peoples often live in areas with a high-risk of climate change, armed conflict, and exploitation by extractive industries.[67]

6.4.2 Opportunities and Entry Points

Engage the representative OPDs of diverse groups of women and girls with disabilities to provide practical advice on how to plan at national and local levels as well as offer information to persons with disabilities on accessible prevention strategies and support, including on GBV. The full, effective, and meaningful participation of women with disabilities in community-led solutions will increase resilience and "build back better" inclusive communities.

ADB stipulates that developing member countries be supported to accelerate the integration of gender equality in national and subnational policies, strategies, and action plans in line with global commitments.[68] Strategies specifically targeted to women with disabilities could include:

- Ensuring gender and disability technical assistance is included in initiatives to reform or support national policies related to climate change, disasters, conflicts, and pandemics. These should draw from the lived experience of women with disabilities to ensure planning encompasses gender, disability-inclusive, and intercultural processes and provisions that are locally adaptable and can influence policies.

- Promotion and support for regular participatory mapping and vulnerability capacity assessments which are gender and disability-inclusive and include women with disabilities in these community processes.

---

[64] Women Enabled International. 2017. *Comments on Draft CEDAW General Recommendation on Gender Related Dimensions of Disaster Risk Reduction in a Changing Climate.* Geneva: OHCHR.

[65] UN. 2016. *CRPD General Comment No. 3 (2016) Women and Girls with disabilities: Situations of risk and humanitarian emergencies (art. 11).* Geneva: UN.

[66] UN. 2012. *General Assembly report of the Special Rapporteur on Violence against Women, its Causes and Consequences, Rashida Manjoo, in accordance with General Assembly resolution 65/187, 3 August 2012.* Geneva: UN. para. 25.

[67] International Disabilities Alliance, Indigenous Peoples with Disabilities Global Network and UN Women. 2020. *Fact Sheet: Indigenous Women with Disabilities.* New York: UN Women. p. 7.

[68] ADB. 2019. *Operational Plan 3: Tackling climate change, building climate and disaster resilience, and enhancing environmental sustainability.* Manila: ADB.

Figure 9: Entry Points to Strengthen Women and Girls with Disabilities' Resilience to External Shocks

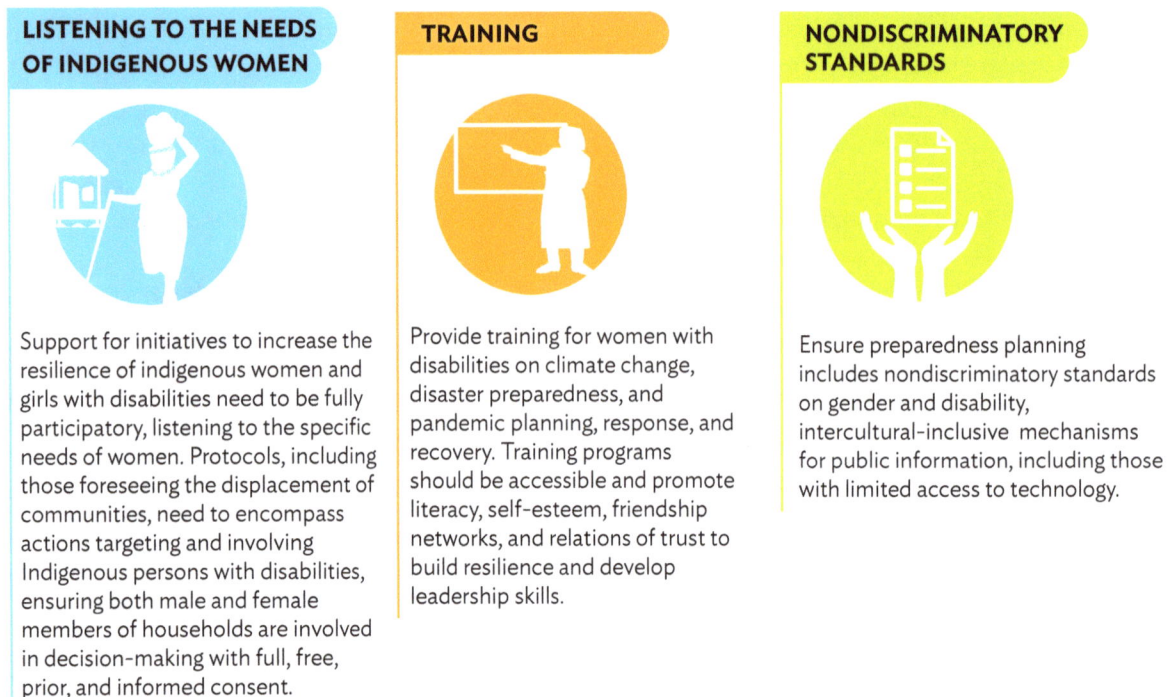

LISTENING TO THE NEEDS OF INDIGENOUS WOMEN

Support for initiatives to increase the resilience of indigenous women and girls with disabilities need to be fully participatory, listening to the specific needs of women. Protocols, including those foreseeing the displacement of communities, need to encompass actions targeting and involving Indigenous persons with disabilities, ensuring both male and female members of households are involved in decision-making with full, free, prior, and informed consent.

TRAINING

Provide training for women with disabilities on climate change, disaster preparedness, and pandemic planning, response, and recovery. Training programs should be accessible and promote literacy, self-esteem, friendship networks, and relations of trust to build resilience and develop leadership skills.

NONDISCRIMINATORY STANDARDS

Ensure preparedness planning includes nondiscriminatory standards on gender and disability, intercultural-inclusive mechanisms for public information, including those with limited access to technology.

Source: Author.

- Building recovery assistance staff's knowledge of discriminatory laws, international and national standards, and the impacts of stigma on the well-being of women and girls with disabilities, and their families and communities.

- Ensuring planning allows for accessible assistance to women with disabilities without them needing to separately claim these rights. This includes accessible treatment and care, mental health and psychosocial support and care services, and support for children with disabilities.

- Employing women with disabilities directly as service providers and personnel providing assistance in times of crisis, as well as acknowledging their skills and knowledge as reference points or coordinators of support for persons with disabilities.

- Promoting and delivering responsive, targeted financial relief and income support for women with disabilities and their carers who are disproportionately impacted by the crisis. This can include preferential access to loans, disaster insurance, and other finance safety nets.

- Implementing targeted measures to protect women with disabilities living in institutional settings who are at heightened risk of neglect, restraint, isolation, and abandonment.[69]

---

[69]   Women's Refugee Commission. 2015. *Including Adolescent Girls with Disabilities in Humanitarian Programs: Principles and Guidelines.* New York: WRC. p. 2.

6.5   Eliminating Harmful Social Norms and Practices and Gender-Based Violence for Women and Girls with Disabilities

It is difficult to separate the impacts of harmful social norms and practices from the impacts of GBV, as many harmful social norms can themselves be forms of violence, and social norms and stereotypes are drivers of GBV. This section outlines the forms of GBV faced by women and girls with disabilities, and the harmful social norms and stereotypes that fuel them. The section on entry points in programming combines both harmful social norms and GBV, as the prevention of GBV must address the underlying causes.

The discrimination and stigmatizing of women and girls with disabilities is possibly the most researched and applied area of programming specifically addressing the nexus of gender inequality and ableism. Significant work has also been done on sexual and reproductive health due to the restrictions placed on women and girls with disabilities. Their denial of these rights is a form of GBV. This is addressed further in section 8.1 Health Sector Guidelines.

6.5.1   Key Issues and Barriers

- The intersection of gender inequality and ableism produce unique experiences of violence and harmful practices for women and girls with disabilities. A study on preventing violence against women and girls with disabilities identified that some forms of GBV are perpetrated against women and girls with disabilities at significantly higher rates. These include disability hate crimes, family violence, domestic violence and intimate partner violence, financial abuse, medical exploitation or abuse, neglect, physical violence, psychological or emotional abuse, restrictive practices, sexual and reproductive coercion or violence, sexual harassment, sexual violence or assault, spiritual and cultural abuse, and technology-assisted violence.[70] Definitions and examples of these types of violence are provided in Appendix 2.

- Other forms of GBV include intentional homicide, infanticide, and "mercy killings," forced psychiatric interventions, neglect, starvation or ill-treatment, forced marriage, and "virgin testing," and "virgin rapes" (particularly for women with albinism who are seen to cure AIDS). Women and girls with disabilities are also highly vulnerable to sex trafficking (particularly women and girls with cognitive impairments and from ethnic and socially marginalized communities), as well as forced labor. In some cases, women are intentionally injured, becoming visibly disabled to increase money from begging. They are also preyed on for the trafficking of body parts and organs which may be driven by superstition.[71]

- From a study of five countries across Africa and Asia looking at intimate partner violence (IPV) and disability for women, it was found that women with disabilities experience IPV at a rate of 44% compared to 26% for women without disabilities. Almost half (45.6%) of the women

---

[70]   Our Watch and Women with Disabilities Victoria. 2022. *Changing the landscape: A national resource to prevent violence against women and girls with disabilities*. Melbourne: Our Watch. pp. 28–31.

[71]   Women Enabled International. 2013. *Statement at the UN Commission on the Status of Women, 57th session, 8 March 2013. Harmful Traditional Practices and Violence against Women and Girls with Disabilities*. Washington, DC: WEI; UN Women. 2017. *Issue Brief: Making the SDGs Count for Women and Girls with Disabilities*. New York: UN Women. p. 2; Women Enabled International. 2019. *Submission by Women Enabled International and Disability Rights International to the Committee on the Elimination of Discrimination against Women on its Elaboration of a General Recommendation on Trafficking in Women and Girls in the Context of Global Migration*. Washington, DC: WEI.

with disabilities experienced sexual IPV compared to 24.2% of women without disabilities.[72] A national safety survey in Australia found 52% of women with cognitive impairments had experienced intimate partner violence since the age of 15, compared with 51% of women with psychosocial impairments, 38% with sensory impairments, and 37% with physical disabilities.[73]

- The *World Report on Disability* reports that girls with cognitive disorders may also be targeted for trafficking in sexual exploitation and begging.[74] Women and girls with disabilities living in residential institutional settings, such as orphanages, group homes, or psychiatric institutions are also at an elevated risk of abuse and trafficking. They can also be exploited though forced labor described as "rehabilitation" or "occupational activity."[75]

- Forced marriage is a form of GBV and differentially impacts on women and girls with disabilities. To address the long-term issues of care or ease the financial burden of women and girls with disabilities, parents in many countries may force their daughters into marriage. In South Asia, the World Bank cites that girls with cognitive or psychosocial disabilities may be forced into early marriage to "cure or improve" their disability, with men sometimes claiming a higher dowry, using their wives for labor or accessing their land. In other cases, women and girls are seen as unfit for marriage, due to shame and perceptions they are not able to have children or conduct household work.[76]

- Stereotypical views of women with disabilities as "unfit" mothers may lead to the termination of parental rights by social service agencies or in child custody and protection proceedings following divorce.[77]

- A study referenced by the World Bank's *Brief on Violence Against Women and Girls with Disabilities* indicated that for women in jails, they were five times more likely to have a psychosocial disability than women not in jail. The brief identified that women and girls with cognitive and psychosocial disabilities were living in jails due to the inadequate capacity of psychiatric services or community-based care facilities. In jails, as with other residential settings, women and girls with disabilities face a higher risk of violence and abuse by other inmates and prison staff, as well as self-harm. They are also more likely to have their legal decision-making rights taken away.[78]

Figure 10 indicates how social norms and stereotypes drive GBV against women and girls with disabilities. It also recognizes additional forms of discrimination generated by disability, gender, and ethnic-related social norms, stigma, and harmful practices which intersect to drive higher rates and other forms of violence (e.g., the withholding of passports for migrant and trafficked women with disabilities).

---

[72] E. Chirwa et al. 2020. Intimate partner violence among women with and without disabilities: a pooled analysis of baseline data from seven violence-prevention programmes. *BMJ Global Health* 2020 5:e 002156. p. 7. bmjgh–2019–002156.pdf (nih.gov).

[73] Research Excellence in Disability and Health. 2020. *Intimate partner violence against people with disability in Australia.* Melbourne: Melbourne Disability Institute.

[74] World Health Organization and the World Bank. 2011. *World Report on Disability.* Geneva: WHO. p. 251.

[75] World Health Organization and the World Bank. 2011. *World Report on Disability.* Geneva: WHO. pp. 1–3.

[76] World Bank. 2019. *Brief on Violence Against Women and Girls with Disabilities.* Washington, DC: World Bank, The Global Women's Institute, Inter-American Bank and the International Center for Research on Women. pp. 7 and 9.

[77] UN Women. 2017. *Issue Brief: Making the SDGs Count for Women and Girls with Disabilities.* New York: UN Women. p. 2.

[78] World Bank. 2019. *Brief on Violence Against Women and Girls with Disabilities.* Washington, DC: World Bank, The Global Women's Institute, Inter-American Bank and the International Center for Research on Women. pp. 13–14.

Figure 10: Conceptual Model of the Intersecting Drivers of Violence against Women and Girls with Disabilities

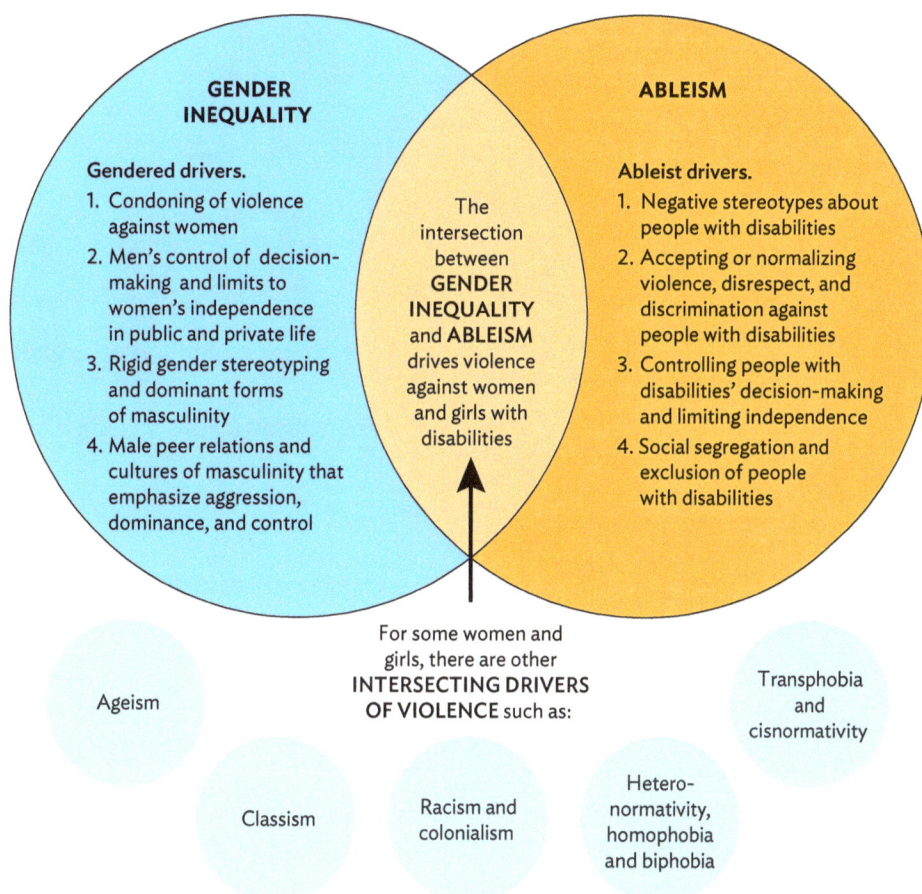

GENDER INEQUALITY

Gendered drivers.
1. Condoning of violence against women
2. Men's control of decision-making and limits to women's independence in public and private life
3. Rigid gender stereotyping and dominant forms of masculinity
4. Male peer relations and cultures of masculinity that emphasize aggression, dominance, and control

The intersection between **GENDER INEQUALITY** and **ABLEISM** drives violence against women and girls with disabilities

ABLEISM

Ableist drivers.
1. Negative stereotypes about people with disabilities
2. Accepting or normalizing violence, disrespect, and discrimination against people with disabilities
3. Controlling people with disabilities' decision-making and limiting independence
4. Social segregation and exclusion of people with disabilities

For some women and girls, there are other **INTERSECTING DRIVERS OF VIOLENCE** such as:

Ageism

Classism

Racism and colonialism

Hetero-normativity, homophobia and biphobia

Transphobia and cisnormativity

Image description: Venn diagram with two intersecting circles- ableism and gender inequality with the area of overlap identifying the intersection as the driver of violence against women and girls. A series of smaller circles point toward the intersection and are labelled as additional forms of discrimination.

Source: Our Watch and Women with Disabilities Victoria. 2022. *Changing the landscape: A national resource to prevent violence against women and girls with disabilities*. Melbourne: Our Watch. p. 36. Reproduced with permission.

- Harmful social and cultural norms faced by women and girls with disabilities include the belief that disability is a "curse" and that persons with disabilities are "possessed" or "evil," and that mothers of children born with disabilities are "witches" or "demonic." They are seen as burdensome to others (i.e., they must be cared for, are a cause of hardship, an affliction, a responsibility, require protection), vulnerable (i.e., defenseless, unsafe, dependent, reliant, unsafe), victims (i.e., suffering, passive, helpless), inferior (i.e., inability, inadequacy, weak and/or worthless), and as hypersexual or sexually abnormal.[79]

---

[79] Women Enabled International. 2013. *Statement at the UN Commission on the Status of Women, 57th session, 8 March 2013. Harmful Traditional Practices and Violence Against Women and Girls with Disabilities*. Washington, DC: WEI; UN. 2012. *UN General Assembly report of the Special Rapporteur on Violence against Women, its Causes and Consequences, Rashida Manjoo. 2012, in accordance with General Assembly resolution 65/187*. Geneva: UN; UN. 2016. *CRPD General Comment No. 3. 2016. Women and Girls with Disabilities*. Geneva: UN.

- These views devalue the basic dignity and autonomy of women and girls with disabilities, and deprive them of basic human rights, including civil and political rights and economic, social, and cultural rights. This is illustrated through the increased scrutiny and prejudicial treatment by social service agencies and assumptions that women with disabilities are unfit mothers. This is often used against women with disabilities in divorce and custody trials, leading them to lose custody and visitation rights with their children.[80]

6.5.2 Opportunities and Entry Points

Our Watch, an Australian organization leading violence against women prevention work, has identified six essential actions for programming to address GBV faced by women and girls with disabilities. These are to:

- Address the underlying social context that gives rise to violence against women and girls with disabilities.
- Challenge the acceptance and normalization of violence against women and girls with disabilities.
- Improve attitudes toward women and girls with disabilities by challenging ableist and sexist stereotypes.
- Promote the inclusion of women and girls with disabilities in all aspects of life.
- Promote women and girls with disabilities' independence, agency and participation in leadership and decision-making; and
- Engage men and boys to challenge controlling, dominant and aggressive forms of masculinity.[81]
- Work with governments to support legal, institutional, and governance reforms to ensure the rights of women and girls with disabilities are enshrined in law and policy aligned with Article 16 of CRPD (*Freedom from exploitation, violence, and abuse*). This includes educational support for women and girls with disabilities and their families and caregivers on how to avoid, recognize, and report instances of exploitation, violence, and abuse.
- Enable women and girls with disabilities to exercise their legal capacity by making their own decisions, with supported decision-making where specifically requested, regarding medical interventions and care. This includes decisions on retaining their relationships and reproductive rights.[82]
- Tackle gender, cultural, and ethnic stereotypes of women and girls with disabilities. Create and promote community campaigns to address gendered disability discrimination and dispel myths against women and girls with disabilities. Include the voices of diverse women with diverse disabilities.[83]
- Promote opportunities and participation for diverse women with diverse disabilities to share ideas, learn and lead, and be included in learning forums, research, and events. Ensure they

---

[80] UN. 2012. *UN General Assembly report of the Special Rapporteur on Violence against Women, its Causes and Consequences, Rashida Manjoo, in accordance with General Assembly resolution 65/187, 3 August 2012.* Geneva: UN.

[81] Our Watch and Women with Disabilities Victoria. 2022. *Changing the landscape: A national resource to prevent violence against women and girls with disabilities.* Melbourne: Our Watch. p. 50.

[82] UN. 2016. *CRPD General Comment No. 3 (2016).* para. 44.

[83] Our Watch and Women with Disabilities Victoria. 2022. *Changing the landscape: A national resource to prevent violence against women and girls with disabilities.* Melbourne: Our Watch.

have the opportunity to participate as trainers, facilitators and researchers, and role models, and that their voices are heard.

- Promote the public participation and profile of diverse women with diverse disabilities to increase visibility of their capacity, skills, and leadership.

- Work with police, prosecutors, and courts to increase awareness of the rights of women and girls with disabilities, the forms of discrimination they face, ensuring the disbelief and dismissal of women and girls with disabilities in the legal system is remedied (footnote 87).

7

Core Elements for Gendered Disability Inclusion across All Programming

This section provides a general outline of some key issues, barriers, entry points, and opportunities in addressing gendered disability inclusion for programming across the whole programming cycle. The next section will focus on a more detailed sector specific approach to address the social sectors of health, education, and social protection, as well as the infrastructure sectors of transport, water security, and urban development.

A critical issue for all projects addressing persons with disabilities as with women and girls with disabilities is consultation in line with the movement's motto "nothing about us without us." This entails listening, learning from, and being guided by the lived experience, expertise, and community leadership of diverse groups of women and girls with disabilities. Recognizing women and girls with disabilities as experts on the issues they face in daily life should be accompanied by an approach that moves beyond only looking at the barriers faced by women and girls with disabilities, but celebrates "disability pride" and supports the inclusion of women and girls with disabilities in all aspects of development including promoting their leadership in activities (see alignment to the ADB road map on disability inclusion in Box 10).

Box 10: Strategic Partnerships to Leverage Impact

The Asian Development Bank (ADB), on its own, cannot achieve disability inclusion or its Strategy 2030 goals. Strategic partnerships with other actors in disability-inclusive development at the global, regional, subregional, and national levels, including Organizations of Persons with Disabilities, can speed up the implementation of Strategy 2030 priorities and magnify the impact of ADB investments in individual countries and at the regional level.

Source: Asian Development Bank. 2022. *Strengthening Disability-Inclusive Development 2021–2025 Road Map*. Manila: ADB. p. 17.

7.1 Government Dialogue

All ADB DMCs have signed up to achieving the SDGs, all but two DMCs have either signed or ratified the CRPD, [84] and they have all endorsed the Incheon Strategy, the Beijing Action Plan, and the Jakarta Declaration. Additionally, all but two DMCs have ratified CEDAW.

---

[84] As of 21 October 2022, Niue and Timor-Leste have taken no action on the CRPD; Bhutan, Tajikistan, and Tonga have signed, but not ratified the CRPD; and all other DMCs have signed and ratified with Uzbekistan becoming a party to the CRPD most recently in 2021. Tonga and Palau have yet to ratify CEDAW.

- Discussions with DMCs can be aligned with government disability and gender policies to understand a partner country's legislative frameworks and the implementation of their commitments to SDGs, CRPD, and CEDAW.
- Seek information on guidelines, building standards, codes, or regulations on minimum universal design for infrastructure and reasonable accommodations in the workplace, cognizant of different needs for diverse women.
- Raise the importance of universal and gender-responsive design with government and other development partners, advocating for inclusion in local laws and policies.

ADB's new resource *Disability Inclusion Brief* identifies provides a clear outline of approaching disability inclusion in the Country Partnership Strategy process. This is outlined in Box 11 and is also spelled out in the document in a specific checklist titled *Disability Inclusion in Country Strategy and Program Activities – are people with disabilities counted, consulted, considered, participating, and benefiting?*

Box 11: Disability Inclusion in the Asian Development Bank Country Partnership Strategy

Analysis of the situation of people with disabilities should be reflected in the main text of the country partnership strategy under the Inclusive Social Development section. Different types of disability should be considered in the analysis, as well as the intersection of disability with other vulnerability factors, including gender and age. The social protection sector road map should also include a subsection on disability. The disability profile needs to be translated into pipeline projects that respond to the concerns of people with disabilities either by ensuring they are identified and explicitly targeted within a project or by designing disability-specific projects. The gender analysis should also reflect considerations of the situation of women and girls with disabilities, including older women with disabilities, as well as gender-specific issues such as gender-based violence and reproductive health as they relate to women and girls with disabilities.

Source: *ADB Disability Inclusion Brief,* p. 15 (unpublished).

7.2   Project Concept and Design

An important initiative in the ADB Strengthening Disability-Inclusive Development 2021–2025 Road Map is the ADB Disability Inclusion Indicator and Marker System in Table 1 with a full explanation outlined in the *ADB Disability Inclusion Brief.*

Table 1: Asian Development Bank Rating System for Disability Inclusion

Rating	Rating Description
3	Principally or significantly disability inclusive
2	Some disability inclusion elements
1	Enabling conditions for disability inclusion, no explicit disability inclusion elements
0	No disability inclusion, no enabling conditions for disability inclusion

Source: ADB. 2022.*Strengthening Disability-Inclusive Development 2021–2025 Road Map.* Manila: ADB, p. 47.

This rating system is in close alignment with the Gender Mainstreaming Categories of ADB Projects (Table 2). The Guidelines for Gender Mainstreaming Categories of ADB Projects provides guidance for specific modalities and technical assistance, examples of gender design features and targets/indicators for ADB's OP2.

Table 2: Asian Development Bank Project Gender Mainstreaming Categories

Category	Description
Category I	Gender equity theme (GEN)
Category II	Effective gender mainstreaming (EGM)
Category III	Some gender elements (SGE)
Category IV	No gender elements (NGE)

Source: ADB. 2021. *Guidelines for Gender Mainstreaming Categories of ADB Projects*. Manila: ADB, p.1.

Both these rating systems will provide essential tools to guide the identification of issues that women and girls with disabilities face that should be addressed and included at the project concept stage. Note that all projects should consider the specific gender and disability exclusion issues in the region or country of programming as stereotypes and harmful social norms women and girls with disabilities face may vary according to the local culture and religious context. Ideally, all staff will build their understanding of a rights-based of disability as it intersects with gender and be ready to engage with government and other partners on these issues when designing projects. However, until such capacity is built, and for activities with focused gender and disability programming, a **gender, disability, and social inclusion specialist** can be included as a design team member or advisor.

Gendered disability inclusion must be clearly addressed within the terms of reference **(TORs)** for project teams and implementing partners to ensure it is embedded in the concept and design phase. The project needs to identify women and girls with disabilities among the target beneficiaries and stakeholders and engage directly with them at the outset. The Washington Group Questions (WGQs) or the WHO Disability Assessment Schedule (WHODAS 2.0) are useful tools to utilize and integrate into design. Project teams must be required to have adequate expertise to address these issues. Contracts should ensure any construction projects align with international **universal design** standards with reasonable accommodations and assistive devices as required. The Australian Department of Foreign Affairs and Trade (DFAT) has developed a *Disability Inclusion in the DFAT Development Program Good Practice Note*[85] and an *Accessibility Design Guide: Universal design principles for Australia's aid program,*[86] an excellent resource.

---

[85]   See https://www.dfat.gov.au/sites/default/files/disability-inclusive-development-guidance-note.pdf.

[86]   See https://www.dfat.gov.au/about-us/publications/Pages/accessibility-design-guide-universal-design-principles-for-australia-s-aid-program.

Adequate budget must be set for gendered disability inclusion, including but not limited to an adequate payment of time for technical services and advice of OPDs and women with disabilities throughout all phases of the program: design, implementation, monitoring, and technical advice of government dialogue and policy reforms. DFAT recommends that 3%–5% of program budgets should be allocated to disability inclusion, including the costs for persons with disabilities and OPDs to participate in and benefit from projects.

As there is little data addressing the specific issues related to women and girls with disabilities, it is necessary to conduct specific **needs assessment** on the issues and barriers facing women and girls with disabilities in the relevant contextual geographical area and/or sector.

A useful resource that may be used in project planning is an *Accessibility Audit* developed by UN Women in 2021,[87] and a *Gender Accessibility Audit Toolkit* developed by UN Women and the National Assembly of People with Disabilities in Ukraine in 2018 which identifies architectural, infrastructural, information, and communication barriers that prevent women and girls with disabilities from fully exercising their human rights and fundamental freedoms.[88] It also includes specific questions on health services for women and girls with disabilities, and questions regarding attitudes of staff.

7.3   Project Implementation

Women with diverse lived experience of disability should be drawn on and be paid for their skills at equal international and national renumeration rates. Unskilled and low-skilled women with disabilities should be **targeted for employment** wherever possible.

Additionally, all training and capacity building activities undertaken should target the inclusion of diverse and underrepresented women with disabilities due to their lack of access of education and training. If any **mentorship or scholarship** projects are offered, actively seek out and liaise with OPDs to facilitate their inclusion with reasonable accommodations. Diverse women with disabilities can also be promoted as expert speakers, members of official delegations, and in high-profile decision-making bodies within projects and at events to support role modelling.

ADB Poverty and Social Assessments could collect disaggregated data and develop deeper analysis with a focus on poor women and girls with disabilities and those who are further disadvantaged, such as those who are Indigenous, from ethnic groups, migrants, refugees, Scheduled Caste, and Tribe. Identifying the key barriers for these women and women who care for family members with disabilities will be a significant step to leaving no one behind in the development process. ADB's *Handbook on Poverty and Social Assessment* provides guidance on addressing poverty, inequality, and exclusion; gender; stakeholders and participation; social risks and vulnerabilities; and institutions and capacity. Each of these areas provide entry points to address the specific issues facing women and girls with disabilities. (See the *ADB Disability Inclusion Toolkit* for disability inclusion in poverty and social assessments and Box 12.)

---

87   To access the *UN Women Accessibility Audit Brief*: https://www.unwomen.org/sites/default/files/Headquarters/Attachments/Sections/Library/Publications/2021/Brief-Accessiblity-audit-en.pdf.

88   To access the *Gender Accessibility Audit Toolkit*: https://www2.unwomen.org/-/media/field%20office%20eca/attachments/publications/2019/gender-accessibility-audit-eng_compressed.pdf?la=en&vs=29.

Box 12: Disability Inclusion in Poverty and Social Assessments

Addressing Disability Inclusion in Asian Development Bank Operations:
Poverty and Social Assessment

As a broad rule of thumb, therefore, if ADB guidance on poverty and social assessment (PSA) is followed, then all operations should be disability-inclusive as people with disabilities will be identified among potential target populations, their situation analyzed, and their additional needs or accommodations considered during scoping studies, initial poverty and social analysis, and other project preparation activities. They will participate, along with other vulnerable or excluded groups of people, in activities that inform the design of the project, safeguarding consultations, or other due diligence activities and measures. Their representative organizations (organizations of persons with disabilities or OPDs) will be consulted and participate in project design activities alongside other key stakeholders. Baseline studies will establish people with disabilities among project target populations and impact channels will be identified for addressing barriers to their ability to benefit from the project alongside other beneficiaries without disabilities. Design and monitoring frameworks (DMFs) will include disability disaggregated indicators and means of verification, including surveys and studies involving people with disabilities and their representative organizations. They will also specify use of universal design standards in all infrastructure and construction projects, and adherence to government disability-inclusive employment quotas or disability-inclusive education policies and other measures for supporting access to education, employment, and livelihoods for people with disabilities.

Source: *ADB Disability Inclusion Brief* (Working title, Unpublished).

Similarly, **ADB Gender Assessment and Action Plans** (GAAPs) need to articulate a stronger approach to intersectionality, addressing how different forms of disability impact diverse women and girls. As GAAPs often include targets for women in employment, training, and other project activities, this could include targets for women with diverse disabilities and include associated reasonable accommodations. The role of women who are the primary carers of family members with disabilities should also be considered in GAAPs.

Disaggregated data should be included relating to sex, age, and **disability (SADD)**. The **Washington Group Questions (WGQs)**[89] have been developed to address the lack of standard indicators across countries on population-based measures of disability. A key feature of the WGQs is the avoidance of the use of the term "disability." It refers to "difficulties" in doing tasks such as walking, seeing, or hearing. The benefit of the WGQs is that they capture more accurate data on disability (often missing from official statistics) as many people do not label or consider themselves to have a disability. The WHO Disability Assessment Schedule (WHODAS 2.0) can also be used. (See the ADB Disability Brief for full details on the WGQs.)

---

[89] See https://www.washingtongroup-disability.com/.

To supplement chronic gaps in national data on SADD, it is important to meet with women with disabilities from OPDs and women's groups which represent a diversity of women and underrepresented groups who are most likely to be left behind in the development process. This can be facilitated through **focus group discussions** in the proposed project areas with diverse women with different types of disabilities. This would ideally include women with disabilities who are poor, in the indigenous or ethnic minority, and older women, as well as young women and women from rural areas. Accessing these women can be facilitated through local women's groups and OPDs that work in the community. They will be able to provide translation in accessible formats and local languages, identify suitable and accessible venues at times the target groups of women are available, and can usually provide communications for sight and hearing impairments, or can access these services locally.

Capacity building for government, counterpart, and project staff should include modules as well as mainstreaming issues of gendered disability as a part of a twin track approach. This includes all gender training ensuring the specific needs of diverse women with diverse abilities are addressed, as well as awareness on gendered disability discrimination and the need to address stereotypes and social norms in line with international standards. All disability inclusion training should include a gender analysis of the different issues for women with disabilities. Best practice would be to commission women with disabilities who are technical specialists to design and run both full training sessions and the specific components for the gender and disability activities.

Discrimination, stigma, and social norms specifically experienced by women with diverse disabilities should be **called out**. This includes advocacy at the highest level of government dialogue, country program development, and policy advice to ensure country policies adhere to the commitments of the **CRPD** and other documents addressed in the section on normative standards. Particular attention should be paid to the issues of GBV and sexual assault and the associated time burdens of the care work that women do for family members with disabilities.

Directly **addressing the stereotypes** of women with disabilities as vulnerable, incapacitated, and unable to function as equal members of society can be done in many ways. These include through programming, funding, and supporting campaigns led by women with disabilities to dispel myths and promoting a social and rights-based model of disability inclusion.

Due to the increased risk and incidence of GBV, it is essential that all projects implement the 2022 ADB Good Practice Note on Addressing Sexual Exploitation, Abuse, and Harassment in ADB-Financed Projects with Civil Works[90] throughout project preparation and project implementation and contract management, especially regarding specific measures to address barriers to reporting by the most marginalized and vulnerable communities, including women and girls with mental and physical disabilities.

---

[90] See GPN on Addressing SEAH in ADB-Financed Projects with Civil Works in Sovereign Operations.

7.4   Monitoring and Evaluation

Ensure the monitoring and evaluation framework uses a **twin track approach** to track progress for diverse women and girls with disabilities throughout all programming, as well as specific indicators formulated to target outcomes for women and girls with disabilities.

Monitoring and evaluation frameworks can include indicators to track SADD and other personal data for women with disabilities which can be identified with consent, and which may be relevant to identifying the program benefits for those most likely to be left behind in the development process.

In addition to the growth in capacity and expertise of ADB staff, contractors should include personnel with **gender, disability, and social development skills** (preferably a woman with disabilities or through a gender-responsive OPD), or team members with technical expertise in the area in the evaluation team. The outcomes and evidence of transformative change for women and girls with disabilities can be referenced in the TOR and structure of the report.

7.5   Checklist for Programming

Table 3: Checklist for Programming

Project Stage	Issues to Address
Project concept and design stage	Budget for gendered disability inclusion aspects of the project, including the identification of women and girls with disabilities among the target beneficiaries and stakeholders and engage directly with them at the outset (see the next two points).
	Consider the inclusion of gender, disability, and social development expertise in design team and needs assessments using the Washington Group Questions (WGQs) if needed to fill national and regional data gaps in the prevalence of disability within a population.
	Include local gender-responsive OPDs at outset of planning (see ADB resource *Deepening Civil Society Engagement for Disability-Inclusive Development Effectiveness in ADB Operations* for a guide on OPDs in the region and consultation processes).
	Consider the inclusion of gender, disability, and social development expertise in needs assessment teams to identify issues and barriers facing women and girls with disabilities in the project geographical and sector context.
	Conduct accessible and culturally sensitive stakeholder discussions with diverse groups of women with diverse disabilities, contracting local women with disabilities (possibly through the OPDs above).
	Ensure gendered disability inclusion is addressed from the outset, at investment concept or design stage.
	Ensure Terms of Reference for Project Teams and implementing partners address gendered disability inclusion within their reportable activities for contracts with references to reasonable accommodations and universal design standards.

continued of next page

Table 3 continued

Project Stage	Issues to Address
Implementation	Payment provided for persons with disabilities and OPDs for the value of their knowledge and technical skills whenever they are consulted and used in an advisory capacity (noting women with disabilities are often expected to provide free advice and they are already juggling multiple roles).
	Prioritize the employment of women with disabilities. Target where possible the employment of women with disabilities. Promote mentorship, scholarship, and other capacity development opportunities.
	Elevate the voices of women with disabilities as expert speakers, delegates, representatives, and as role models of the program or project.
	Ensure data collections are robust, highly diverse and representative of diverse women and girls with diverse disabilities and their carers.
	Formulate Gender Assessment and Action Plans targeted to how different forms of disability impact women and girls.
	Disaggregate data for sex, age, and disability (SADD).
	Utilize the WGQs to fill national and regional data gaps in the prevalence of disability within a population.
	Use focus group discussions and other consultative and participatory techniques to fill data gaps and understand local contextual issues from people with lived experience.
	Undertake gender and disability awareness training, facilitated by gender and disability experts, preferably women with disabilities, where possible.
	Address the stereotypes, harmful practices and behaviors that perpetuate stigmatization and discrimination, including celebrating disability as normal human diversity.
	Take seriously the actual and perceived risk and consequence of GBV, adhering to best practice guidelines for its prevention, reporting, and response.
	Ensure implementation of the Good Practice Note on Addressing Sexual Exploitation, Abuse, and Harassment in ADB-Financed Projects with Civil Works
Monitoring, review, and evaluation	Ensure monitoring and evaluation frameworks include indicators to consistently disaggregate and track SADD and other relevant identifiers.
	Use a twin track approach to track progress for diverse women and girls with disabilities.
	Require the inclusion of personnel with gender and disability technical skills, preferably women with disabilities.
	Ensure evaluations document evidence of transformative change for women and girls with disabilities.

ADB = Asian Development Bank, GBV = gender-based violence, OPD = Organization of Persons with Disabilities.

Source: Developed specifically for these guidelines by the author Suzette Mitchell.

7.6   Useful Resources

Useful resources that provide guidance on universal design, accessibility, reasonable accommodations, and appropriate measures in disability inclusion that specifically include reference to the needs of women and girls include:

- AusAID. 2013. *Accessibility Design Guide: Universal Design Principles for Australia's Aid Program*. Canberra: AusAID. https://www.dfat.gov.au/about-us/publications/Pages/accessibility-design-guide-universal-design-principles-for-australia-s-aid-program.
- UN Women. n.d. In Brief: *Accessibility Audit*. New York: UN Women. https://www.unwomen.org/en/digital-library/publications/2021/07/brief-accessibility-audit.
- UN Women. n.d. *Accessibility and Reasonable Accommodation*. New York: UN Women. https://www.unwomen.org/en/digital-library/publications/2021/10/brief-accessibility-and-reasonable-accommodation.
- R. Wima and J. Sandhu. 2010. *Integrating Appropriate Measures for People with Disabilities in the Infrastructure Sector*. Eschborn: GTZ. https://unipd-centrodirittiumani.it/en/diritti_umani_disabili/Integrating-appropriate-measures-for-people-with-disabilities-in-the-infrastructure-sector/179.

In addition, Women Enabled International has produced two good practice guides.

- Women Enabled International. n.d. *ACCESS: Good Practices – Social Media*. Washington, DC: WEI. https://womenenabled.org/reports/access-good-practices-social-media/.
- **Women Enabled International. n.d.** *ACCESS: Good Practices – International Meeting Checklist*. **Washington, DC: WEI.** https://womenenabled.org/reports/good-practices-international-meetings-checklist/.

8 Sector Guidelines

The following sets of guidelines sequentially address the social sectors of health, education, and social protection. This is followed by the infrastructure sectors of water security, transport, and urban development. Each sector guide identifies the key issues and barriers facing women and girls with disabilities, followed by potential opportunities for entry points in programming. A set of sample indicators are provided which are aligned with the ADB *Toolkit on Gender Equality Results and Indicators*[91] which is a highly respected resource in the gender equality sector. The final section includes an applicable case study and a set of annotated resources.

8.1 Health

Disability arises from a health condition that may be genetic, disease-driven, or caused by social and environment factors (i.e., lack of access to food, safe water, unsanitary conditions, or violence, accidents, including road accidents, or trauma or stressful events). Women and girls, especially those living in poverty and/or groups with multiple socially marginalized identities are at a higher risk of social and environmental factors. This leads to higher rates of disability for women and girls than men and boys. Many people associate disability with physical impairments that can be seen or sensory impairments (hearing and sight), which become obvious on communication. The neglect of people living with cognitive and psychosocial disabilities is widespread in the context of development projects with little research or attention to these disability types, their differential causes, or presentations in women and girls, especially in lower-income countries. UN Women reports that almost 42% of disability from neuropsychiatric disorders in women is due to depression compared to 30% among men.[92] Psychosocial disabilities can result from the impacts of gender discrimination, the intersection of gender and other discriminations (i.e., racial, age, those faced by people of diverse SOGIESC, indigenous, scheduled caste, tribe, and others), gender norms and stereotypes, poverty, hunger, malnutrition, violence, and overwork and care burdens.[93] Addressing mental health issues for women and girls is increasing globally; however, it is not systemically addressed in low- to middle-income countries (LMICs) in the Asia and Pacific region.

Autism spectrum disorder (ASD) is globally considered to affect more boys than girls with rates in boys four times higher than girls. Recent research suggests, however, that the rates for girls have

---

[91] ADB. *Tool Kit on Gender Equality Results and Indicators*. https://www.adb.org/documents/tool-kit-gender-equality-results-and-indicators.

[92] UN Women. 2019. *Issues Brief: Making the SDGS Count for Women and Girls with Disabilities*. New York: UN Women. pp. 3-4.

[93] J. Astbury. 2001. Gender disparities in mental health. *Mental Health. Ministerial Round Tables 2001, 54th World Health Assembly*. Geneva: WHO.

been consistently underestimated as the criterion for diagnosing ASD has historically been based almost entirely from studies of boys.[94] Studies show that ASD presents differently in girls with traits commonly unrecognized, especially due to girls increasingly "camouflaging" their symptoms to avoid social exclusion and presenting higher verbal skills than boys. This aligns with the findings of a review of medical manuals recommended by 20 of the most prestigious universities in Europe, the United States, and Canada that found "images of white men predominate in western anatomy textbooks, which present them as a 'universal model' of the human being."[95]

One area where significant research has occurred for women and girls with disabilities is in the area of sexual and reproductive health (SRH) and GBV.[96] This is due to significant violations of the SRH rights of women and girls with disabilities, and the considerably higher prevalence and diverse forms of GBV they experience. GBV is a critical health issue not only for the psychosocial impacts on all women, but for the physical health issues inflicted, which increases the rates of disability among women and girls of all ages.

The Special Rapporteur on the rights of persons with disabilities presented a report to the General Assembly in 2017 titled the *Sexual and Reproductive Health and Rights of Girls and Young Women with Disabilities*. The report documents various abuses of human rights suffered by women and girls with disabilities, including a high prevalence of forced and involuntary sterilization. This is often considered to be in their best interests to prevent menstruation and pregnancies due to perceptions they are "unfit for parenthood."[97] The report states: "Forced sterilization is an unacceptable practice with lifelong consequences on the physical and mental integrity of girls and young women with disabilities that must be immediately eradicated and criminalized."[98]

8.1.1   Issues and Barriers for Women and Girls with Disabilities in Health

Table 4: Issues and Barriers for Women and Girls with Disabilities in Health

Key Issue	Evidence
Heightened impact of COVID-19 on health of women and girls with disabilities.	• A 2021 study *Experiences of women with disabilities in the Asia-Pacific region during COVID-19* raised safety concerns of women and girls with disabilities living in institutions. It cites an OPDs trying to get information about COVID-19 rates within institutions but found no data was being collected. Participants in the study reported unverified information on reported deaths within institutions. The study also identified the long-term impacts of the COVID-19 pandemic on women with disabilities' psychosocial well-being, mental health, reduced well-being from lockdowns, and increased hospitalization for severe mental health relapses.[a]

continued of next page

---

[94]   M. Szalavitz. 2016. Autism—It's Different in Girls: New research suggests the disorder often looks different in females, many of whom are being misdiagnosed and missing out on the support they need. https://www.scientificamerican.com/article/autism-it-s-different-in-girls/. 27(2). pp. 48–55.

[95]   Plataforma SINC. 2008. Medical Textbooks Use White, Heterosexual Men as a 'Universal Model. *ScienceDaily*. 17 October 2008. https://www.sciencedaily.com/releases/2008/10/081015132108.htm.

[96]   For more specific information on the risks, prevalence, and forms of GBV faced by women and girls with disabilities, see section 6.5.

[97]   General Assembly Seventy-second session. 14 July 2017. Report of the Special Rapporteur on the rights of persons with disabilities on *Sexual and reproductive health and rights of girls and young women with disabilities*. para. 29.

[98]   General Assembly Seventy-second session. 14 July 2017. Report of the Special Rapporteur on the rights of persons with disabilities on *Sexual and reproductive health and rights of girls and young women with disabilities*. para. 30.

Table 4 continued

Key Issue	Evidence
Women and girls acquire disabilities due to gender-related health issues.	• About 20 million women each year acquire a disability because of pregnancy and childbirth, mainly due to a lack of access to appropriate health care services.[b] Limited data is available, but from the countries where data is collected, it is suggested that 29% of births by women with disabilities are not attended by a skilled health worker, and 22% of married women with disabilities having an unmet need for family planning.[c] • Increased rates of violence for women and girls with disabilities result in higher rates of disability.
Women and girls with disabilities lack access to sexual and reproductive health (SRH).	• Women and girls with disabilities in various countries across the Asia and Pacific region are assumed not to require SRH information,[d] or it may also not be available in accessible formats, exposing women and girls with disabilities to the risks of unintended pregnancies, sexually transmitted diseases, and GBV.[e] These women and girls with disabilities are at risk of forced contraception and sterilization procedures (note c) and are often subject to substituted decision-making and denial of personal autonomy.[f] • The CRPD Committee stated in 2016 (note c) that women and girls with disabilities have the right to choose the number and spacing of their children, as well as the right to have control over and decide freely and responsibly on matters related to their sexuality, including sexual and reproductive health, free of coercion, discrimination and violence.[g] However, the choices of women and girls with disabilities, especially those with psychosocial or intellectual disabilities are often ignored, with their decisions substituted to third parties, including legal representatives, service providers, guardians, or family members, thus violating their rights under Article 12.[h]
Limited accommodation of health facilities for women and girls with disabilities.	• Women and girls with disabilities receive less screening for breast and cervical cancer than women without disabilities due to a lack of targeted health promotion and prevention campaigns, and a lack of appropriate physical accommodation.[i] • Health care facilities and equipment, including mammogram machines and gynecological examination beds, are often physically inaccessible for women with disabilities (note d).
Social norms and inequality cause barriers for women and girls with disabilities to access health care.	• Physical, financial, legal, attitudinal and information barriers are an obstacle for persons with disabilities accessing health care, increasing the exposure of women and girls with disabilities and their families to illness. • With low levels of literacy and education, women with disabilities have more difficulty accessing health care. They rarely know their legal rights and may have difficulty accessing and asserting their rights in stigma-free and suitable health care services. • Health care workers have been reported as lacking sensitivity, responsiveness, courtesy, and support for women and girls with disabilities through misinformation of their capacities and capabilities (note c).

COVID-19 = coronavirus disease, CRPD = Convention on the Rights of Persons with Disabilities, GBV = gender-based violence, OPD = Organization of Persons with Disabilities.

[a] UN Women. 2021. Experiences of women with disabilities in the Asia-Pacific region during COVID-19. New York: UN Women. p. 2 and 3.

[b] Pacific Women Shaping Pacific Development. 2021. *Thematic Brief: Inclusion of Pacific Women with Disabilities.* Canberra: DFAT.

[c] UN 2020. Sixth session of the Working Group on the Asian and Pacific Decade of Persons with Disabilities, 2013–2022: Review of recent progress in the implementation of the Asian and Pacific Decade of Persons with Disabilities, 2013–2022. Bangkok: UN Economic and Social Commission for Asia and the Pacific.

[d] UN Women. 2019. *Issues Brief: Making the SDGS Count for Women and Girls with Disabilities.* New York: UN Women. pp. 3–4.

[e] See, for example, CRPD/C/MEX/CO/1. para. 50b, CRPD General Comment No. 3 (2016) Article 6: Women and Girls with disabilities. B: Sexual and reproductive health and rights, including respect for the home and the family (Articles 23 and 25).

[g] CRPD General Comment No. 3 (2016) Article 6: Women and Girls with Disabilities. para. 23.

[h] CRPD General Comment No. 3 (2016) Article 6: Women and Girls with Disabilities. para. 25.

[i] WHO. 2014. *Eliminating forced, coercive and otherwise involuntary sterilization: An interagency statement OHCHR, UN Women, UNAIDS, UNDP, UNFPA, UNICEF, and WHO.* Geneva: WHO.

[j] CRPD/C/GC/2, para. 40. Also see, for example, CRPD/C/DOM/CO/1. para. 46.

8.1.2   Potential Opportunities and Entry Points for Health Programming for Women and Girls with Disabilities

- Addressing the health and well-being of women and girls with disabilities requires comprehensive policy reforms targeting availability, adaptability, accessibility, affordability, and quality, with gender- and disability-specific awareness-raising and training for health and service providers, and improved data collections disaggregated by age, type of disability, gender, ethnicity, and geography.

- Where projects include policy-based loans, policy reforms should align with CRPD General Comment 3 on *Women and Girls with disabilities* which states that *"all women with disabilities must be able to exercise their legal capacity, making their own decisions, with support when desired with regard to medical and/or therapeutic treatment. Women with disabilities should be autonomous in decisions regarding: their fertility, reproductive autonomy, their right to choose the number and spacing of children, to consent and accept a statement of fatherhood, and the right to establish relationships. Restricting or removing legal capacity can lead to forced interventions, such as: sterilization, abortion, contraception, female genital mutilation, or surgery, or treatment performed on intersex children without their informed consent and forced detention in institutions."*[99] Policies and regulations for SRH services should include safely screening women with disabilities (as with all women) for GBV, with referral to accessible services with trauma-informed approaches.

- All health care services need to be accessible to women and girls with disabilities, as with all persons with disabilities. Health campaigns need to include materials that are inclusive of women and girls with disabilities' needs, including images with understandable local language guides addressing their particular needs. Due to increased poverty levels for women and girls with disabilities, free or low-cost services should be provided.

- Health workers should be provided with information about the potential health and social consequences of COVID-19 for immunocompromised women and girls with disabilities, and how lockdowns may increase risk of GBV due to close confinement with family members.

- Barriers to meeting the basic health care needs of women and girls with disabilities include lack of access to information and disability accommodation, as well as income, education, lack of transport and ability. Services must be inclusive of Indigenous and ethnic groups, including scheduled castes and scheduled tribes, people of diverse SOGIESC, migrants, and refugees. Rights-based and intercultural approaches should be used in consultation with Indigenous women with disabilities, including different modes of questioning responsive to the language styles and structures of Indigenous and linguistic groups.[100]

- Health care services and products needed by women and girls with disabilities because of their disability should be classified as essential services. This may include mental health care, pain management, rehabilitation, and equipment like hearing aids, wheelchairs, diapers, and catheters.

---

[99]   CRPD/ General Comment 3. para. 44.

[100]   International Disabilities Alliance, Indigenous Peoples with Disabilities Global Network and UN Women. 2020. *Fact Sheet: Indigenous Women with Disabilities.* p. 6.

- In times of disaster and crisis, menstrual supplies should be considered essential and distributed with other nonfood items, such as gender-responsive disability-inclusive WASH or dignity kits.[101]

- Menstrual supplies should consider the needs and preferences of women and girls with different types of disabilities. In 2021, UNICEF developed a tip-sheet to support and identify practical entry points for meeting the needs of women and girls with disabilities when they menstruate. The tip sheet addresses combating stigma and discrimination by applying approaches of social and behavior change communication, providing access to accurate and timely information, safe, private, reliable infrastructure and supplies, including accessible transportation and access to affordable and appropriate sanitary protection materials.

- Hospital and clinic policies need to explain that women and girls with disabilities have a right to be accompanied by a support person or interpreter to health care appointments, even if local regulations or health clinic or hospital rules limit patient accompaniment. This is essential for SRH appointments and in labor, delivery, and postpartum wards. Where telehealth or online services are available, accessible platforms (e.g., phone calls, online platforms) should include sign language interpretation or other accommodations to enable access for women and girls with disabilities.

- Capacity building and training plans need to be put in place to support all health workers, including SRH workers, to provide rights-based care for women with disabilities, implement telehealth services, ensure accessibility including to accommodations, and ensure continuity of care. Health care workers need to consider the full range of impairments women and girls with disabilities experience when communicating with them, including using plain language for women and girls with intellectual disabilities.

COVID-19 has highlighted the importance of working toward deinstitutionalization and ensuring that people with disabilities can live independently to address long-term mental health issues for women and girls with disabilities. Providing accessible and inclusive psychosocial and peer support should be a critical element of health plans for all women and girls with disabilities, especially for those with psychosocial disabilities.[102]

---

[101] World Bank 2020. *Pivoting to Leveraging Lessons from the COVID-19 Crisis for Learners with Disabilities.* Washington, DC: World Bank. p. 47.

[102] UN Women. 2021. *Experiences of women with disabilities in the Asia-Pacific region during COVID-19.* New York: UN Women. p. 6.

8.1.3   Sample Indicators for Health Systems to Address the Needs of Women and Girls with Disabilities throughout the Project Cycle

Note: the indicators include a mix of potential outcome and output indicators to encompass the whole project cycle from project preparation, design, implementation, review, and evaluation.

Table 5: Sample Indicators for Health Systems to Address the Needs of Women and Girls with Disabilities throughout the Project Cycle

Issue	Indicators
Decision-making, leadership, participation, legal and institutional reform	
Consulting with international and national OPDs run by women and/or working with women's rights health specialists will assist in the development of relevant and effective strategies to address their health needs.	Number of consultations with women-led OPDs or OPDs with a focus on gender and health rights in the project design, implementation, monitoring, and review. Number of and type of initiatives designed and implemented from the direct advice of women-centered OPDs and women with disabilities involved in the consultation process for the project or program. Percentage of WWD holding managerial or leadership positions and/or providing advisory roles.
Reforming health policy can bring it in line with international standards for the rights of women and girls with disabilities, especially relating to sexual and reproductive health (SRH).	Number of policy reforms in the health sector aligning with Convention on the Rights of Persons with Disabilities (CRPD) Comment 6 on women and girls with disabilities ensuring legal capacity to take their own decisions on retaining their fertility, reproductive autonomy, right to choose the number and spacing of children, to consent and accept a statement of fatherhood, and the right to establish relationships. Restrict or remove legal capacities that can facilitate forced interventions, including sterilization, abortion, contraception, female genital mutilation, surgery, or treatment performed on intersex children without their informed consent and forced detention in institutions (for policy-based loans).
Human development	
Ensuring the health concerns of women and girls with disabilities are addressed and the sector meets international standards for those most likely to be left behind in health needs.	Number of health initiatives that mainstream the needs for women and girls with disabilities throughout design and implementation. Number of stand-alone initiatives or components to address a priority need that liaise with or contract to an OPD focusing on the rights of women and girls with disabilities, with women with diverse disabilities directly leading the initiative. Number and type of initiatives that address the specific cognitive and psychosocial needs of women and girls with disabilities. Number of women and girls with disabilities who report increased support, safety. and strategies to assist their impairments, including those with psychosocial and cognitive disabilities.
	Number and percentage of budget for health initiatives directly benefiting women and girls with disabilities, including: Number and amount of reasonable accommodations that have been incorporated into health initiatives, including maternity and gynecological needs. Number of health initiatives using rights-based intercultural approaches designed by women with diverse disabilities. Number of health publications or communication campaigns that are focused on gender- and disability-specific discrimination. Number of health publications or communication campaigns that are available in oral, easy reading formats, braille and sign language distributed and targeted through OPDs to address the specific needs of women and girls with disabilities. Results of a review to assess the outreach and usage of the publications and communications campaigns listed above.

continued of next page

Table 5 continued

Issue	Indicators
Decreasing time poverty and drudgery	
Including support for women as carers of family members with disabilities can reduce the time burden and address the physical and mental exhaustion of carers.	Number of women who are carers of family members with disabilities who report improved knowledge to assist their care role and report accessing respite through survey data.
	Number of initiatives that provide support for carers of family members, especially for women and girls with cognitive and psychosocial disabilities. This can include health initiatives that enable free or low-cost respite for women as carers of family members with disabilities to address their own mental and physical health needs.
	Number of time saving initiatives or new technology or tools developed to support women and girls with disabilities and/or women as carers of people of disabilities.
	Percentage of increase of formal service provisions for the care of persons with disabilities.
Economic empowerment	
Increasing the employment of women with disabilities in the health sector both increases their economic empowerment and enables the health sector to draw from their specific knowledge related to the health of women and girls with disabilities.	Number of increase of women with disabilities who are employed in health services.
	Number and percentage of women with disabilities who are employed in health services working within the project, tracked in monitoring and evaluation framework over the period of the program.
	Number and percentage of women with disabilities who report receiving assistance from program initiatives.
	Number of women with disabilities with paid advisory roles in project activities.
	Amount and percentage of budget identified for specialist technical assistance provided by women with disabilities or gender and disability health experts aligned with equal pay for international and national consultants.
	Number of health training courses with quotas for women with disabilities providing all necessary reasonable accommodations.
	Number of women with disabilities engaged in health sector internships.
Increasing resilience to external shocks, eliminating harmful social norms and violence against women and girls with disabilities	
Working to ensure SRH rights of women and girls with disabilities will increase their human rights in line with international standards in the CRPD.	Number of gender- and disability-specific training for all health services, including SRH and GBV service providers and for police and justice sector personnel addressing the rights of women and girls with disabilities aligned to international United Nations standards.
	Number of health and justice providers that report increased understanding of the needs, concerns, and forms of discrimination facing women and girls with disabilities, and report using strategies and accommodations in subsequent work.
	Number of accessible forms of SRH and GBV information, education, and communication materials for women and girls with disabilities distributed.
	Percentage of increase of women and girls with disabilities who report increased awareness and understanding of their SRH rights.

GBV = gender-based violence, OPD = Organization of Persons with Disabilities, WWD = Women with Disabilities.

Source: Developed specifically for these guidelines by the author Suzette Mitchell.

8.1.4 Case Study on Health

Box 13: Samoa Case Study: Reproductive Health and Rights for Women and Girls with Disabilities

In Samoa, women with disabilities face particular stigma from community members, family members, and health care providers relating to having children. This attitudinal barrier seems to be primarily driven by stereotypes that women with disabilities will give birth to a child with disabilities and assumptions that the woman will be unable to care for the child. For women with disabilities already raising children, some reported feeling supported by their village community, while others felt isolated and discriminated against by their community, teachers, and medical providers.

In 2020, the United Nations Population Fund (UNFPA) Pacific engaged the organization of persons with disabilities Women Enabled International (WEI), the Pacific Disability Forum (PDF), and the national disability civil society organization Nuanua O Le Alofa (NOLA) to conduct an assessment on sexual and reproductive health issues and rights, GBV, and access to essential services for women and young people with disabilities in Samoa. The lived experience of several young deaf women from the Samoan study's focus group interviews are expressed below identifying the barriers, violence and stigma these women have faced:

"Yes [I believe I was targeted because of my disability]. They say I am deaf. They say if they violate me (sex me), I don't go tell anyone. They think we are stupid."

"When I was pregnant, I was so looking forward to taking care of my baby because I was experienced in taking care of my other cousins and siblings. However, I didn't know my parents had pre-arranged for a cousin of mine to take my baby and care for her. My family told me I cannot look after my baby. I felt so sad."

"[Following my rape], my cousin took me to [the] police. She was unfamiliar with [the] procedures. My cousin didn't understand my signs [and the] police didn't quite understand. We went to police station in Savaii, the police didn't file our case. We couldn't find the records. The police got sacked."

"I am not sure about parts of the body. I do not know that sort of information... I don't know anything about sexual or body parts. I see neighbor girls having babies, I don't know how it happened."

The findings indicated the need for women and girls with disabilities to be able to access brief and clear messaging about their rights. WEI, a nongovernment organization (NGO) led by and for women with disabilities, developed a Know Your Rights guide. Some of the sample messaging developed appears below.

continued of next page

Box 13 continued

EXAMPLE: You have the right to be included in and to be able to understand the information featured in any **GBV COVID-19 awareness-raising campaigns** addressing the increased risk of violence during COVID-19 restrictions and about available services.

EXAMPLE: You have a right to be **accompanied by a support person or interpreter to healthcare appointments,** even where local regulations or health clinic or hospital rules limit patient accompaniment.

EXAMPLE: You have the right to have the disability related **support services** you require to be classified as essential services. This right is important to enable you to live independently and to not have to rely on your family or institutional settings for essential support services and basic needs like food, water and housing.

EXAMPLE: Women, girls, and gender nonconforming persons with disabilities must be consulted in the government's assessments of GBV during the COVID-19 pandemic and **funding and programming** assigned accordingly.

EXAMPLE: Women, girls, and gender nonconforming persons with disabilities must be included in the collection of **data disaggregated by both gender and disability** on the impact of COVID-19 on GBV.

EXAMPLE: You have the right—even during COVID-19 lockdowns or stay-at-home orders—to **leave your house to escape violence,** seek help from the police, or access health and GBV services.

COVID-19 = coronavirus disease, GBV = gender-based violence.

Sources: UNFPA, Women Enabled International and Pacific Disability Forum. 2022. *Women, Girls, and Gender Non-Conforming People with Disabilities — Know Your Rights! Gender-based violence and sexual and reproductive health during the COVID-19 pandemic in the Pacific Region.* Fiji: UNFPA. p. 4; UNFPA, Women Enabled International and Pacific Disability Forum. 2021. *Women and young people with disabilities in Samoa: Needs assessment of sexual and reproductive health and rights, gender-based violence, and access to essential services.* Apia, Samoa: UNFPA. pp.11,15,16, and 24.

8.1.5   Useful Resources

Pacific Disability Forum. 2014. *Toolkit on Eliminating Violence Against Women and Girls with Disabilities In Fiji.* Suva: DFAT.

This toolkit was developed by a number of OPDs working with women and girls with disabilities in relation to violence. The research investigated the barriers for women and girls with disabilities reporting violence, as well as accessing medical care and counselling. The toolkit was developed by the Pacific Disability Forum with the Fiji Disabled Peoples Federation with input from CBM – Nossal Institute Partnership for Disability-Inclusive Development. It is a training kit and provides facilitators a guide with tools and strategies to present sessions using a Power, Privilege, and Gender Relations framework. It identifies the barriers faced by women and girls with disabilities that experience violence and encourages participants to identify local strategies eliminate violence against women and girls with disabilities.

UNFPA and WEI. 2018. *Women and Young Persons with Disabilities: Guidelines for Providing Rights-Based and Gender-Responsive Services to Address Gender-Based Violence and Sexual and Reproductive Health and Rights.* New York: UNFPA.

The guidelines provide practical guidance to ensure SRH and GBV services are inclusive and accessible for women and young persons with a variety of disabilities. Targeted interventions are included to meet disability-specific needs in all settings, including humanitarian emergencies.

UNFPA and Women Enabled International. 2021. *The Impact of COVID-19 on Women and Girls with Disabilities: A Global Assessment and Case Studies on Sexual and Reproductive Health and Rights, Gender-Based Violence, and Related Rights.* Bangkok: UNFPA.

This resource pack is designed for development workers, policy officials, aid agencies, and other stakeholders active in COVID-19 response and recovery. It covers planning, response, and recovery, which can simultaneously be used to address other forms of crisis and promote inclusive policies and practices for women and girls with disabilities.

UNFPA, Women Enabled International and Pacific Disability Forum. 2021. *Women and Young People with Disabilities in Samoa: Needs Assessment of Sexual and Reproductive Health and Rights, Gender-Based Violence, and Access to Essential Services.* Apia, Samoa: UNFPA.

UNFPA Pacific partnered with Women Enabled International (WEI) and the Pacific Disability Forum to conduct three disability needs assessments to identify barriers that prevent women and young people with disabilities being able to fully realize their SRH rights, fully access SRH services, and to prevent GBV. The assessments were conducted in Fiji, Samoa, and Vanuatu. The research found that women and young people with disabilities require easily digestible information about their rights. As a result, DFAT funded UNFPA to work again with WEI to develop a Know Your Rights guide in partnership with the Pacific Disability Forum.

Women Enabled International. 2018. Facts: *The Sexual and Reproductive Health and Rights of Women and Girls with Disabilities.* Washington, DC: WEI.

Women and girls with disabilities are just as likely to be sexually active and have the same SRH needs as women and girls without disabilities. Due to multiple and intersecting forms of discrimination on the basis of gender and disability, however, women and girls with disabilities face unique and pervasive barriers to full realization of their SRH and rights.

8.2   Education

A study conducted as a part of the UN's Girls Education Initiative (UNGEI) *Still left behind: Pathways to inclusive education for girls with disabilities* identified girls with disabilities as often unseen and unheard making them the least likely to benefit from education initiatives in low-income countries. The study expressed concern regarding the neglect of girls with disabilities in education policy and practice, citing disability and gender issues as significant factors for their exclusion and yet not considered simultaneously.[103]

---

[103]   UN Girls Education Initiative and Leonard Cheshire. 2017. Still left behind: Pathways to inclusive education for girls with disabilities. New York: UNGEI.

8.2.1 Issues and Barriers to Education for Women and Girls with Disabilities

Table 6: Issues and Barriers to Education for Women and Girls with Disabilities

Key Issue	Evidence
Global data on inequality in education for women and girls with disabilities.	• Statistics for primary school children indicate 52.9% completion for girls without disabilities, 50.6% for boys with disabilities and only 41.7% for girls with disabilities.[a] • This statistic is even lower in early childhood education where a study of 42 counties found only 18% of girls with one or more functioning difficulties attended an early childhood education program compared to 28% of girls without functional difficulties.[b] • United Nations Educational, Scientific and Cultural Organization (UNESCO) reports the global literacy rate for women with disabilities may be as low as 1%.[c]
Social norms and discrimination create barriers for the education of girls with disabilities.	• Girls with disabilities face multiple financial, social and cultural, and accessibility issues in accessing schooling. This can be due to lower social expectations of girls with disabilities as it is assumed they will not be productive members of society, whereas boys with disabilities are still viewed as potentially contributing to household finances.[d] • Girls with disabilities may be kept inside the home due to embarrassment and may not have their birth registered which means they will not be visible to the education system. They may also experience less hours of care, food, and access to health care (note d). • Girls with disabilities experience heightened rates of bullying and teasing by their peers based on their disability and gender (note d) and are at heightened risk of sexual violence in special education institutional settings.[e] • Girls with disabilities are commonly restricted from participating or receiving comprehensive sexual education (CSE) due to misconceptions that they are asexual and/or should not be sexually active. Girls with disabilities may not attend schools when CSE is delivered, and materials are published in alternative formats (note 3). (See section 8.1 Health and section 8.2 Education sector guidelines).
Disability has different impacts on girls in schools.	• Physical barriers for women and girls with disabilities accessing education are due to the lack of modified educational resources, accessible transportation and adequate toilets (see section 8.4 Water Security and Water Sanitation and Hygiene and section 8.5 Transport Sector Guidelines). Boys with disabilities have greater access to assistive technology and rehabilitation. • Evidence shows that boys with cognitive and psychosocial learning disabilities present differently to girls, and show higher rates of impulsivity, aggression, and hyperactivity leading to diagnosis and access to educational accommodation. Girls with these same disabilities exhibit less obvious behaviors which often includes inattentiveness as well as presenting as quiet and nondisruptive. Autistic girls are consistently underdiagnosed (see section 8.1 Health Sector Guidelines) resulting in their lack of access to educational support.[f]
Women with disabilities face barriers accessing further education.	• Women who are carers of children with disabilities are often deprived of the time to attend further education. • Women and girls with disabilities do not have equal access to technical vocational education training to attain the vocational skills to enter formal sector jobs with greater financial security and access to career opportunities (note f). However, there is evidence to show that when young women with disabilities do access higher education, they have higher completion rates than young men with disabilities. • There is a lack of women with disabilities as teachers and as role models promoted in the media to inspire girls with disabilities and they are generally invisible in teaching resources.

[a] World Health Organization and the World Bank. 2011. World Report on Disability. Geneva: WHO.

[b] UN Women. 2022. *Progress on the Sustainable Development Goals: The Gender Snapshot 2022*. New York: UN Women. p. 4.

[c] CRPD. Some Facts about Persons with Disabilities. http://www.un.org/disabilities/convention/facts.shtml.

[d] S. Ortoleva. 2015. Yes, Girls and Women with Disabilities Do Math! An Intersectionality Analysis. A. Hans, ed. *Disability, Gender and the Trajectories of Power*. Thousand Oaks, California: Sage Publishing.

[e] Women Enabled International. 2021. Factsheet: The Right to Education for Women and Girls with Disabilities. Washington, DC: WEI.

[f] UN Girls Education Initiative and Leonard Cheshire. 2017. Still left behind: Pathways to inclusive education for girls with disabilities. New York: UNGEI.

8.2.2 Potential Opportunities and Entry Points for Programming

Governments have an international obligation to provide inclusive education, recognizing all learners have unique characteristics, interests, abilities, and particular learning needs (footnote 107).

- A process of "nothing about us without us" in partnership with OPDs working at the intersection of gender equality, education, and disability rights is essential in the design and implementation of education programming initiatives. This can include funding for girls with disabilities networks in schools and in communities.

- Engage and work with women with disabilities networks to design school and community awareness raising campaigns to address stereotypes, stigmatization, and bullying of girls with disabilities, and promote positive role models of local national and international women with disabilities who have attended university and attained senior professional positions.

- Ensure gender- and disability-specific learning programs are developed inclusive of cultural learning styles and languages of girls with disabilities most underrepresented in formal schooling structures, specifically girls with disabilities who are Indigenous, poor, from ethnic groups, scheduled caste or tribes, migrant and refugee, or other socially disadvantaged groups.

- Promote and provide early learning, primary and secondary curricula, and assessment tools to address the less obvious and different learning needs of girls with disabilities. This will require education systems to have the specialist knowledge to identify diverse presentations of learning disabilities for girls and specialist teacher training to modify curriculum, materials, and support girls with disabilities. For example, a modification for autistic girls is to provide a quiet space to decompress sensory overload from loud and bright classrooms. Another is to provide clear written short instructions rather than long descriptive oral directions (footnote 107).

- Take positive measures to ensure effective access to inclusive education, including access to safe transport, integrated schools (not separate "special education"), access to learning accommodations, and accessible WASH facilities with menstrual hygiene facilities for girls.

- Targets on attendance and learning must contain specific indicators disaggregated by sex and types of disability, age, and ethnicity.

- Apply an intersectional equity-focused gender and disability lens to budgeting and resource allocation to expose and account for all costs that disproportionately affect girls with disabilities.[104]

- Progress toward inclusive and gender-responsive education should be tracked with the WGQs[105] as well as ensuring data collection and analysis is disaggregated by sex, type of disability, and other relevant local identifiers such as Indigeneity, ethnicity, caste or tribe among other groups of girls with disabilities who may be traditionally underserved by the education system.

---

[104] Pacific Women Shaping Pacific Development. 2021. *Thematic Brief: Inclusion of Pacific women with disabilities.* Canberra: Australian Aid.

[105] See: https://www.washingtongroup-disability.com/question-sets/.

- TVET programs can provide quotas and scholarships for women and girls with disabilities. Without TVET programs that attract equal numbers of women with disabilities, opportunities for employment will remain low.[106]
- Cross-sector consultation, coordination, and collaboration must be strengthened to overcome the multilayered barriers to education faced by girls with disabilities, including across health, child protection, and WASH sectors.

8.2.3 Sample Indicators for Education Systems to Address the Needs of Women and Girls with Disabilities

Table 7: Sample Indicators for Education Systems to Address the Needs of Women and Girls with Disabilities

Issue	Indicators
Decision-making, leadership, participation, legal and institutional reform	
Ensuring gender-responsive disability inclusion provisions in education sector policies and plans will increase equitable access for the education of girls with disabilities.	Number of policy initiatives and reforms that refer specifically to the needs of girls with disabilities, including but not limited to identifying the differential learning disabilities of boys and girls; equity of access of learning accommodations; and accessible sex segregated water, sanitation, and hygiene (WASH) facilities with access to menstrual hygiene needs (for policy-based loans).
Allocating project resources to address the inequities faced by girls with disabilities in the education system will ensure girls' needs are not overlooked.	Amount and percentage of budget identified to meet the needs of girls with disabilities in education programming.
Women with disabilities and OPDs with expertise in the education of girls with disabilities have a wealth of knowledge to draw from in local and national decision-making to reverse social and cultural barriers.	Number of women with disabilities who are participants of, or lead, monitoring activity. Number of women with disabilities who self-report satisfaction with the process used to consult them on the design of programs. Number of specific initiatives addressing the needs of girls with disabilities that have been adopted in the program from the advice of OPDs and women with disabilities.
Human development	
Teacher training and capacity building is an effective strategy to address the learning needs of girls with diverse disabilities.	Number of specialist in-service and preservice teacher training sessions that increase capacity of school staff (especially welfare and learning support staff) to identify diverse presentations of learning disabilities for girls and provide skills to modify curriculum, materials, and support girls with disabilities. Percentage of girls and women who are identified with learning disabilities disaggregated by infancy, early childhood, primary, secondary. and/or tertiary education.

continued of next page

---

[106] UN. 2020. Sixth session of the Working Group on the Asian and Pacific Decade of Persons with Disabilities, Review of recent progress in the implementation of the Asian and Pacific Decade of Persons with Disabilities, 2013–2022. Bangkok: UN Economic and Social Commission for Asia and the Pacific. para. 10.

Table 7 continued

Issue	Indicators
Girls have increased access to diagnosis of learning disabilities and are subsequently provided with reasonable accommodations.	Percentage of girls with disabilities with access to gender sensitive teaching assistance in the classroom (in primary, secondary. and tertiary education).
Decreasing time poverty and drudgery	
Increase attendance of girls with disabilities in the formal schooling system.	Number and annual percentage increase of girls with disabilities attending school. Percentage of girls with disabilities successfully completing schooling segregated by year level.
The provision of safe accessible transport and basic WASH facilities with access to menstrual hygiene is essential for girls with disabilities to be able to attend school.	Number of WASH facilities installed in schools for girls with disabilities with accessibility, adequate privacy, space, and resources for menstrual hygiene management (note this aligns with indicator in WASH sector).
Economic empowerment	
Girls with disabilities rarely see women with disabilities in teaching and leadership roles which limits their access to role models.	Number and percentage of women vs men with disabilities serving as teachers in schools identified by level of seniority.
Increase attendance for women with disabilities in technical and vocational education and training (TVET).	Percentage of male and female students with disabilities in TVET sectors, including science, technology, engineering, and mathematics.
Access for women with disabilities in tertiary institutions.	Number and percentage of quotas provided for women with disabilities to conduct university degrees.
Eliminating harmful social norms, violence against women and girls with disabilities. and increasing resilience	
Reduced incidents of bullying, harassment. and abuse of girls with disabilities in schools.	Percentage of in-service and preservice teacher training curricula that include and promote approaches of nondiscriminatory gender- and disability-specific inclusive education. Percentage of teachers trained report an increased understanding of the complex barrier girls with disabilities face in learning and have adopted modifications in the classroom. Number of schools initiating and adopting antibullying and inclusion campaigns to educate school community (teachers, parents. and students).
Girls with disabilities access comprehensive sexual education.	Attendance rate for girls with disabilities in sexual education classes.

= number, % = percent, $ = United States dollar, OPDs = Organizations of Persons with Disabilities.
Source: Author.

8.2.4 Case Study on Education

Box 14: Education Case Study: Vocational Training for Women with Disabilities in the Lao People's Democratic Republic

Lao Disabled Women's Development Center (LDWDC) is a nonprofit organization approved by the Lao Ministry of Social Welfare and Labour. It is staffed by disabled women for disabled women. The organization was founded in 1990 by Chanhpheng Sivila who grew up with 11 brothers and sisters. At the age of 3, she contracted polio. The illness affected her left leg and spine, and she was not permitted to attend school. Not one to be pushed around, Chanhpheng stole her sister's uniform and went to school anyway. She has since graduated from Rattana Collage with a Bachelor of Business Administration and Political Management.

Image description: Four women with disabilities sitting at desks signing with their hands during a sign language class. (photo from Lao Disabled Women's Development Center). Disability accessible explanation of image

Since 2014, and in partnership with the Association for the Deaf, LDWDC has trained 20 women as qualified sign interpreters. When the program began, there were only two professional sign language interpreters working in the Lao People's Democratic Republic (Lao PDR). This meant health, legal, and education services were unable to provide sign language interpretation, creating a significant barrier to essential services and leading to social exclusion. Chanhpheng notes the program not only creates sustainable livelihood opportunities for women with disabilities, but also provides an essential service for deaf people throughout the country.

Most of the women with disabilities who are selected for study come from poor, rural areas of the Lao PDR, many are members of minority ethnic groups, and over 80% have lost one or both of their parents. The sign language interpretation course runs over a year. Chanhpheng says "students are provided with safe housing together in a dormitory, appropriate equipment, meals, and free time within a supportive and nurturing community. We also facilitate access to health care and rehabilitation which is often the first time these women have been to the hospital or had any rehabilitation aids or supports." Some of the graduates are now working with deaf associations, others teach classes at LDWDC, and many have returned to the countryside to assist local people who have never previously had the ability to communicate with others. The LDWDC works with the Ministry of Education to assist the women to gain access to literacy skills and graduate from primary school since many, especially those from the countryside, have never attended school.

Other vocational training run by LDWDC includes leadership training for women with disabilities; English and Lao language; computer skills, accessing the internet, and various computer packages, including PowerPoint; social work; finance; sewing; paper making and handicrafts. All the women also receive training in disability law, rights, and the CRPD. This training is also provided to the wider disability community, government, and civil society.

CRPD = Convention on the Rights of Persons with Disabilities.
Source: Lao Disabled Women's Development Center website http://laodisabledwomen.com/#.

8.2.5   Useful Resources

UN Girls Education Initiative and Leonard Cheshire. 2017. *Still left behind: Pathways to inclusive education for girls with disabilities.* New York: UNGEI.

The report provides a synthesis of the understanding of barriers to education for girls with disabilities and brings together evidence of effective or promising program approaches that address these barriers specifically for girls with disabilities.

UN Girls Education Initiative and Leonard Cheshire. 2021. *Leave no girl with disabilities behind: Ensuring efforts to advance gender equality in education are disability-inclusive.* New York: UNGEI.

This advocacy brief from the UN Girls' Education Initiative (UNGEI) and Leonard Cheshire, outlines a framework for advocacy on inclusive education with a focus on girls with disabilities. It provides an overview of global education for girls with disabilities highlighting the key challenges and barriers they face in accessing inclusive and gender-responsive education. Case studies are provided; however, these are all from African countries.

United Nations Children's Fund. 2021. *Seen, counted, included: Using data to shed light on the well-being of children with disabilities.* New York: UNICEF.

This resource aims to fill a gap in providing reliable and comprehensive data to track the inclusion of children with disabilities in development. It builds on data from over 1,000 sources. It documents the scale and characteristics of children with disabilities and begins to shed light on the types of adversity they often face. Internationally comparable data from 43 economies is used to look at 60 indicators of child well-being, including nutrition and health, access to water and sanitation, protection from violence and exploitation, education, and life satisfaction.

Women Enabled International. 2021. *Fact Sheet: The Right to Education for Women and Girls with Disabilities.* Washington, DC: WEI.

Despite having the same rights to education as their male counterparts and nondisabled peers, girls with disabilities are the most excluded group of children from all educational settings from primary school to higher education settings due to multiple and intersecting forms of discrimination on the basis of both their gender and their disability. However, existing laws, policies, and programs do not adequately address the various educational barriers faced by women and girls with disabilities.

World Bank. 2019. *Equity and inclusion in education in world bank projects: Persons with Disabilities, Indigenous Peoples, and Sexual and Gender Minorities.* Washington, DC: World Bank.

The paper focuses on persons with disabilities, indigenous peoples, and sexual and gender minorities who experience various forms of disadvantage, inequity, exclusion, and discrimination in education. It looks at the issues and challenges for each group and addresses strategies for schools, as well as enabling the policy environment to support inclusion and nondiscrimination in education and in all spheres of life.

8.3   Social Protection

Ensuring gender and disability is included in social protection is specifically addressed in SDGs 1 and 10. SDG1 on ending poverty in all its forms everywhere includes target 1.3.1: "proportion of population covered by social protection floors/systems, by sex, distinguishing children, unemployed persons, older persons, persons with disabilities, pregnant women, newborns, work-injury victims and the poor and the vulnerable." SDG10 on reducing inequality within and among countries includes targets:

- 10.1 "universal access to social protection cash benefits related to care and care services will support income growth among the bottom 40 per cent of the population;"
- 10.2 "promote the social, economic and political inclusion of all, irrespective of age, sex, disability, race, ethnicity, origin, religion or economic or other status;"
- 10.3 "fiscal, wage and social protection policies for care workers and unpaid carers will contribute to ensuring equal opportunities and reducing inequalities of outcome;" and
- 10.4 "progressively achieve greater equality."

Social protection for people with disabilities need to consider the basic cost of living in addition to adequate health assistance and the costs for accessing reasonable accommodations which may entail disability-specific equipment, support services, and rehabilitation. It is also important to note indirect extra costs due to lower income due to barriers in employment and education. These issues all impact women and girls with disabilities, as with men and boys; however, their needs may not be as visible, or considered, such as the economic impact of mothers conducting unpaid care work for family members with disabilities which restricts their access to income generation.

The ADB Briefing *Disability and Social Protection in Asia* states that disability-inclusive social protection must ensure access to (i) mainstream social protection programs that aim to reduce poverty or provide adequate income in case of contingency, and (ii) disability-targeted programs where being recognized as having a disability is the main criterion for access to the program. This document identifies the building blocks of social protection for people with disabilities in Figure 11 noting income security can cover specific disability pensions, old-age pensions or minimum income protection, while ensuring any of these forms of pension or social protection schemes cover disability-related costs and support services and support allowances. This aligns with the approach this set of guidelines takes which is that mainstream services, such as social protection should address their specific gendered needs, as well as specifically targeted approaches. where necessary, such as for carers of people with disabilities, who are predominantly women.

The World Bank's revised social protection policy, *Charting a course towards universal social protection: resilience, equity, and opportunity for all,* states that social protection systems are designed for the "average" client in mind with a critical need to consider how vulnerable groups can be excluded from social protection systems. It specifically references women, poor people, people living in isolated and remote areas, refugees, immigrants and Indigenous people, persons with disabilities, and other vulnerable individuals and families facing social risks. It considers a range of strategies to address this such as multidimensional assessment to identify the complex needs of the individuals or households, social audits, citizen and community scorecards, beneficiary surveys, adaptations (such as hiring staff from excluded groups to build trust and reduce stigma) and recommends that program administrators deliberately and proactively reach out to vulnerable populations who may otherwise be overlooked.

Figure 11: The Building Blocks of Social Protection for People with Disabilities

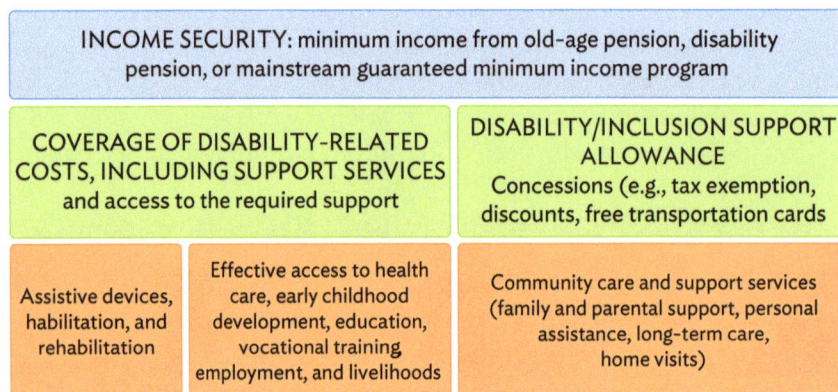

INCOME SECURITY: minimum income from old-age pension, disability pension, or mainstream guaranteed minimum income program

COVERAGE OF DISABILITY-RELATED COSTS, INCLUDING SUPPORT SERVICES and access to the required support

DISABILITY/INCLUSION SUPPORT ALLOWANCE
Concessions (e.g., tax exemption, discounts, free transportation cards

Assistive devices, habilitation, and rehabilitation

Effective access to health care, early childhood development, education, vocational training employment, and livelihoods

Community care and support services (family and parental support, personal assistance, long-term care, home visits)

Sources: Adapted from C. Knox-Vydmanov et al. 2021. *Social Protection and Older Persons with Disabilities*. United Nations Children's Fund (UNICEF), International Labour Organization (ILO), United Nations Partnership on the Rights of Persons with Disabilities (UNPRPD), HelpAge International, and Asian Development Bank; ADB. 2021. *ADB Briefs, No. 203: Disability and Social Protection in Asia*. Manila: ADB. p. 2.

This includes addressing the needs of those who need care for their vital support, as well as lessening the responsibility of care that usually falls on women.[107]

It can be assumed that the rates of access to social protection is significantly lower for women with disabilities; however, there is no global data which specifically looks at the access to social protections for women with disabilities. Separate data exists for women, and for persons with disabilities, but not specifically for women with disabilities. The lack of disaggregated data in social protection for sex, age, and disability is increasingly being addressed through census data using WGQs or WHODAS2 to provide more reliable prevalence data. However, due to social registers rarely disaggregating this data, it is not possible to understand who the recipients of social protection measures are.

It can be assumed that the rates of access to social protection is significantly lower for women with disabilities than either of these groups, considering the higher levels of poverty, lower levels of education and literacy, health, awareness of government programs, and physical access to grant offices. This is particularly the case where social protection is heavily reliant on social security or insurance schemes linked to formal employment.

The COVID-19 pandemic has highlighted the need for universal social protection. Prior to COVID-19, 26.5% of women globally had legal access to comprehensive social protection as opposed to 34.3% of men.[108] The SDG Data Portal indicates over 90% of persons with disabilities were excluded from social protection systems in countries within Asia and the Pacific (where data was available). The lowest rates

---

[107]   World Bank. 2022. *Charting a course towards universal social protection: Resilience, equity, and opportunity for all*. Washington, DC: World Bank. pp. 87–88.

[108]   UN Women. 2022. *Social Protection: Major gaps laid bare*. New York. https://www.unwomen.org/en/hq-complex-page/covid-19-rebuilding-for-resilience/social-protection.

(with less than 5% of persons with disabilities accessing social protection) were in Myanmar,[109] Cambodia, the Philippines, and Türkiye; in contrast to 100% in Kazakhstan, Georgia, Azerbaijan, Armenia, and Mongolia.[110] Another limitation is that some countries only include those who work in the formal economy and their families in their social protection systems. This excludes women with disabilities who may be unemployed or who predominantly work in the informal economy. Even when women with disabilities may be able to access these schemes, they often do not know they exist or how to access them, may not have bank accounts to receive them, or have additional barriers in communicating with grant officers.[111]

8.3.1 Issues and Barriers for Women and Girls with Disabilities in Accessing Social Protection

Table 8: Issues and Barriers for Women and Girls with Disabilities in Accessing Social Protection

Key Issue	Evidence
Women with disabilities experience heightened difficulties in access to timely social protection during the COVID-19 pandemic.	A United Nations (UN) Women study identified that although some women with disabilities in the Asia and Pacific region received government support during COVID-19, it was often too slow to arrive.[a] Some women with disabilities had not been correctly registered prior to the pandemic, rendering them ineligible for support during the pandemic, some were unable to travel to register, while others were eligible for support, but this was provided specifically to male household heads.[b] A positive learning was that women with disabilities were a strong source of support for each other. OPDs also provided information for women in their communities to facilitate their access to government support (note b).
Formal procedures for social protection create exacerbated difficulties for women with disabilities in accessing programs.	The classification and registration of persons with disabilities is unclear in many countries, making access less clear for women with disabilities. Additionally, the design of the eligibility criteria and qualifying conditions and the process for enrolment and registration are difficult for women with disabilities to understand and access (note b). Difficulty obtaining official documentation registration due to costs, discrimination, and stigma (preference not to register girls with disabilities), early marriage (preventing marriage registration), as well as for refugees, Indigenous, internally displaced women with disabilities, and women from ethnic groups who lack official documentation.[c]
Women with disabilities experience inequitable access to social protection systems due to social norms and inequality.	Lack of awareness of benefits or services, or difficulty accessing these due to their physical, sensory, cognitive and psychosocial impairments, sociocultural barriers (stigma and discrimination against women with disabilities), lack of transport, cost of transport, or their dependency on others to assist their access to the benefits.
Women with disabilities can be marginalized by the digitization of social protection systems.	Digital technology and mobile banking have enabled millions of people to access social protection services, and for some women with disabilities, digital technologies can be preferable to in-person engagement as it enables anonymity, may avoid discrimination and stigma, and may increase reporting of safeguarding issues and grievance procedures. However, many women with disabilities have low literacy and digital literacy and are less likely to own or have access to digital devices (e.g., phones) and their own bank accounts.

COVID -19 = coronavirus disease, OPD = Organization of Persons with Disabilities.

[a] UN Women. 2021. Experiences of women with disabilities in the Asia-Pacific region during COVID-19. New York: UN Women.

[b] UN Women. 2021. *Experiences of women with disabilities in the Asia-Pacific region during COVID-19.* New York: UN Women. p. 4.

[c] Social Protection Approaches to COVID-19: Expert Advice (SPACE). 2020. *Inclusive Information Systems for Social Protection: Intentionally Integrating Gender and Disability.* London: FCDO, GIZ and DFAT. p. 4.

---

[109] Effective 1 February 2021, ADB placed a temporary hold on sovereign project disbursements and new contracts in Myanmar.

[110] UN and ADB. 2019. *Accelerating progress: An empowered, inclusive and equal Asia and the Pacific.* Bangkok: UNESCAP. p. 15.

[111] United Nations. 2018. *Disability and Development Report Realizing the Sustainable Development Goals by, for and with persons with disabilities.* New York: UN Department of Economic and Social Affairs. pp. 3 and 41.

8.3.2   Opportunities and Entry Points for Programming

These suggestions represent a diversity of initiatives that could be used to address the critical needs of women with disabilities in formal social protection systems. It has drawn on various authoritative sources, which at times have been modified to the specific needs of women with disabilities.

- Avoid austerity cuts to welfare programs that disproportionately target women with disabilities.[112]
- Offer free, subsidized, or sliding-scale fees for services and medicines or equipment for women with disabilities.
- Expand and invest in quality public and community based social services, including food and housing security programs for women with disabilities.
- Implement targeted measures to protect women with disabilities and those with additional vulnerabilities living in institutional settings as they face a heightened risk of neglect, restraint, isolation, and abandonment.[113]
- Provide universal health care for women with disabilities and expanded affordable or free care services, products, and medicines for women caring for family members with disabilities.
- Provide direct compensation to women with disabilities working in the informal economy or to women who care for relatives with disabilities through cash transfers, in-kind support services or priority access to food, housing, and other types of support. This should include tailored support to women and girls with disabilities to access emergency aid, as well as interventions to fight GBV.[114]
- Perpetrators of sexual abuse for women and girls with disabilities may be their caregiver. Social protection systems should include initiatives to prevent GBV within programs and ensure safe housing and support to survivors.
- Ensure or provide technical assistance to facilitate grievance processes in social protection systems disaggregating data by sex, age, and disability. Provide assistance for tailored communications mechanisms for diverse women with disabilities to access information on grievance processes and build-in feedback loops to analyze complaints for women with disabilities to inform ongoing accessibility and inclusion.[115]

The 2018 *Disability and Development Report: Realizing the Sustainable Development Goals by, for and with Persons with Disabilities* identified specific entry points that can facilitate gendered disability inclusion in social protection:

- Include costing in the benefits for women with disabilities to address the barriers they encounter in the process of registering for entitlements. Provide accessible financial services.

---

[112] UN Women. 2022. *Social Protection: Major gaps laid bare.* New York. https://www.unwomen.org/en/hq-complex-page/covid-19-rebuilding-for-resilience/social-protection.

[113] UN. 2020. Policy Brief no. 69: *Leaving no one behind: the COVID-19 crisis through the disability and gender lens.* New York: UN United Nations Department of Economic and Social Affairs. p. 3.

[114] UN. 2020. Policy Brief no. 69: *Leaving no one behind: the COVID-19 crisis through the disability and gender lens.* New York: UN United Nations Department of Economic and Social Affairs. p. 2.

[115] Social Protection Approaches to COVID-19: Expert Advice (SPACE). 2020. *Inclusive Information Systems for Social Protection: Intentionally Integrating Gender and Disability.* London: FCDO, GIZ, and DFAT.

- Include costings related to disability-related products and services supplemented with training and support for women with disabilities to work.

- Develop and implement training programs for grant officers on the barriers women with disabilities experience when accessing social protection services and engage women with diverse disabilities to enable grant officers to understand their different contexts. Strategies can then be developed for gendered disability-inclusive service delivery to maximize access to benefits.[116]

Social Protection Approaches to COVID-19: Expert Advice (SPACE) argue that while eligibility criterion for social protection programs is ultimately a policy decision, data from social assistance information systems can be used to:

- Prioritize the inclusion of women with disabilities as a criterion for eligibility in programs or giving increased scoring or weight to women and girls with disabilities, and other vulnerable categories during means or proxy means testing;

- Tailor the overall benefit or service package and transfer amounts to the additional (multiple and varied) needs of women with disabilities;

- Adjust systems to compensate for care responsibilities which are disproportionately taken on by women through recognizing non-income costs, such as time spent on care or domestic responsibilities, ability to access services, markets, and others.

SPACE identifies other entry points for programming, including:

- Ensuring registration questionnaires and application forms are inclusive of gender and disability categories.

- Easing the burden of registration and application by reducing the direct, indirect, and opportunity costs faced by women with disabilities. This could include one-stop shops and/or decreased requirements for documentation.

- Conducting an accessibility audit for user-facing interfaces with accessibility experts (including women with disabilities) to test and assess digital solutions.

- Providing in-person engagement to access services via trusted partners such as social workers, health workers, and OPDs working with women. This is critical to outreach and prioritizes dignity and continuity of care over efficiency.

- Using assistive technologies for online, mobile, and other technology-based outreach, serving the specific needs of women with disabilities. This could include automated voice messages for those with visual impairments or who are illiterate, a sign language video for those with hearing impairments, or easy-to-read formats for women with cognitive or psychosocial disabilities. Alternatively, use trusted local information "intermediaries" (such as OPDs working with women, social workers, or health workers) for digitally driven mass campaigns.[117]

---

[116] United Nations. 2018. *Disability and Development Report Realizing the Sustainable Development Goals by, for and with persons with disabilities.* New York: UN Department of Economic and Social Affairs. pp. 5, 45–46.

[117] Social Protection Approaches to COVID-19: Expert Advice (SPACE). 2020. *Inclusive Information Systems for Social Protection: Intentionally Integrating Gender and Disability.* London: FCDO, GIZ, and DFAT. pp. 2, 20, 31.

8.3.3   Sample Indicators for Social Protection Systems to Address the Needs of Women and Girls with Disabilities

Table 9: Sample Indicators for Social Protection Systems to Address the Needs of Women and Girls with Disabilities

Issue	Indicator
Decision-making, leadership, participation, legal and institutional reform	
OPDs and organizations of women with disabilities can play a critical role in ensuring appropriate social protection schemes when they are meaningfully consulted and included in programming.	Number of discussions initiated with OPDs led by or working with diverse groups of women with disabilities. Number of initiatives that have consulted with women with disabilities or OPDs to provide information and advice on effective and feasible mechanisms for inclusion in social protection services. Number of specific consultations undertaken with diverse groups of women with a range of disabilities in impoverished geographical locations. Number of women with disabilities included in the design, implementation, and monitoring of the program identifying age, Indigeneity or ethnic group, and type of disability.
Increasing women with disabilities' representation throughout all levels of decision-making in the social protection sector can lead to increased understanding of, and initiatives to address the needs of women with disabilities in social protection.	Number and percentage of women with disabilities on social protection decision-making mechanisms.
The collection of sex, age, and disability data (SADD) in social protection by national governments will align with standards set by the Convention on the Rights of Persons with Disabilities and the Sustainable Development Goals.	Assessment of social protection data disaggregated by sex, poverty, age, and disability status has informed project design. Number of initiatives or services that directly address, support, and track SADD in social protection.
Policy reform plays an important role for women with disabilities and women as unpaid carers of disabled family members to access social protection services.	Number of social protection policy reforms that identify the specific needs of diverse women with disabilities and the role of women as carers of family members with disabilities.
Human development	
Increasing access to social protection for women with disabilities and women providing unpaid care to family members with disabilities will improve the health of families, access to education for girls and access to employment for women	Number of girls who are newly attending, or returning to school since their family has received social protection. Number of women with disabilities self-report improved nutritional and health status.
Decreasing time poverty and drudgery	
Targeted relief and income support for women as carers of family members with disabilities may provide essential time to engage in economic activities and/or increase their general well being	Results of costing studies that address the unpaid labor women contribute to care of persons with disabilities at the household and community level with an assessment of the costs to the economy for these carers not being economically active.

continued of next page

Table 9 continued

Issue	Indicator
Economic empowerment	
Eliminating discrimination against women with disabilities and including women with disabilities as social protection service providers will increase women's ability to access social protection.	Number of training sessions for grant officers that include information on the discrimination of women and girls with disabilities, and knowledge on reasonable accommodations. Number of women with disabilities trained in management roles in the social protection sector. Percentage of additional support provided to women with disabilities to offset costs of disability needs.
Ensuring equity of access for women with disabilities in social protection (aligned to the ADB Social Protection Categories) will increase their ability to obtain social protection. • Pensions • Health insurance • Other social insurance (unemployment and disability insurance) • Welfare assistance, such as cash or in-kind transfers • Child welfare • Assistance to the elderly • Health assistance (tax funded benefits) • Disability benefits • Skills development and training • Public works programs, such as cash for work or food for work	Percentage of women with disabilities comparative to men with disabilities accessing pensions. Percentage of women with disabilities comparative to men with disabilities accessing health insurance. Percentage of women with disabilities comparative to men with disabilities accessing other social insurance. Percentage of women with disabilities comparative to men with disabilities accessing welfare assistance. Percentage of women with disabilities comparative to men with disabilities accessing assistance to the elderly. Percentage of women with disabilities comparative to men with disabilities accessing health assistance. Percentage of women with disabilities comparative to men with disabilities accessing disability benefits. Percentage of women with disabilities comparative to men with disabilities accessing skills development and training. Percentage of women with disabilities comparative to men with disabilities accessing public works programs, such as cash for work or food for work.
Eliminating harmful social norms, violence against women and girls with disabilities. and increasing resilience	
Inclusive and nondiscriminatory public information and communication enables women with disabilities to access essential information on social protection.	Number and type of accessible formats of information provided on social protection services tailored to the specific needs of women with disabilities and their forms of impairment. Number and percentage of women with disabilities who report satisfaction with process to access social protection support.

\# = number, % = percent, ADB = Asian Development Bank, OPD = Organization of Persons with Disabilities.

Source: ADB. 2019. *The Social Protection Indicator for the Pacific: Assessing Progress*. Manila: ADB, p. 2. Case Study on Social Protection.

8.3.4   Case Study on Social Protection

Box 15: Lived Experience Case Study: Social Protection in Tonga

The Ma'a Fafine Mo e Famili (MFF) Early Intervention Program (EIP) began in 2012, funded by the Government of Japan and administered by by the Asian Development Bank (ADB) for a project called Social Protection of the Vulnerable in the Pacific.

Matelita Fataua lies quietly in bed, covered with a light wool blanket. Her caregiver, Puatiasia Fatai, strokes her hair gently before getting up to tidy the room and prepare lunch.

Matelita is 81 years old and suffered a stroke 3 years ago, which left her bedridden. Her daughter works full-time and has children of her own to take care of. There simply is not enough time in a day to earn a living, raise children, and provide the full-time support that Matelita needs to stay healthy and happy. Tonga's elder care program is designed to help in exactly these circumstances.

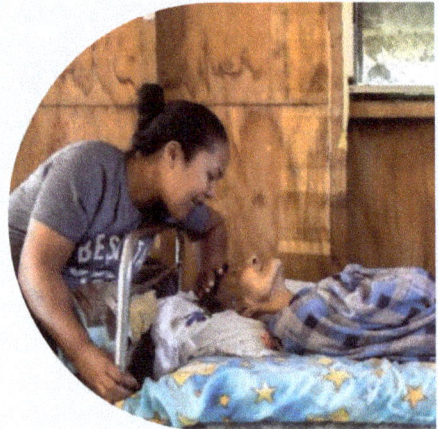

Image description: Matelita Fataua is lying in bed with her caregiver, Puatiasia Fatai, leaning over the bed in conversation with her.(photo by Eric Sales).

Since 2018, Puatiasia has become a loving part of the Fataua household. She visits almost every day for several hours and cares for Matelita as if she were family, helping her eat, use the restroom, wash her clothes, and keep her mind active. Puatiasia earns a living by giving back to the Tongan community. "My mom also got support from MFF's elderly care program. That's how I heard about it," reflects Puatiasia. "[My mom's] caregiver was so helpful when she was sick that when my mom passed away, I told MFF I wanted to help families with similar needs. I've been doing this ever since."

Formal social protection structures like the elder care program and EIP are not replacing informal support—they are enriching it. They integrate with the community and enable it to provide more comprehensive support to those in need.

The project was designed to (i) identify social protection gaps in the Cook Islands, the Marshall Islands, and Tonga; and (ii) support the respective governments in piloting new solutions. In Tonga, the project came at a time when formal social safety nets were still in their infancy and introduced solutions that are still in place today. Crucially, ADB's support engaged the government and local civil society organizations (CSOs) like MFF to ensure strong community ownership and sustainable results.

Tonga's Ministry of Internal Affairs—in large part through its Social Protection and Disability Division—has played an essential role in shaping the direction of social protection programs and advocating for vulnerable people in recent years.

Source: ADB. 2020. *Empowering the Vulnerable in Tonga: A Success Story on Social Protection Services*. Manila: ADB.

8.3.5 Useful Resources

Social Protection Approaches to COVID-19: Expert Advice (SPACE). 2020. *Inclusive Information Systems for Social Protection: Intentionally Integrating Gender and Disability.* London: FCDO, GIZ, and DFAT.

This resource considers disability as one of many additional identities women may hold, including older women, youth, refugee, migrant, Indigenous, LGBTI, and other minority groups. While the resource below is specifically targeted to women with disabilities, this resource refers to the need for disaggregated data by sex, age, and disability. It also refers to the need for gender and disability-sensitive and transformative social protection involving gender, disability, and protection specialists throughout the program cycle. It suggests project staff could develop a network and learning platform between actors working on gender, disability, social protection, humanitarian response, and protection issues.

SPACE. 2020. *Strengthening Gender Equality and Social Inclusion (GESI) During the Implementation of Social Protection Responses to COVID-19.* London: FCDO and GIZ.

This document highlights the key gender equality and social inclusion considerations to be considered in the implementation of social protection, with a specific focus on cash transfers, in response to COVID-19. It provides guidance on how to ensure that the delivery of programs is gender-sensitive, equitable, inclusive, and where possible, transformative. This document can also be read alongside the SPACE Gender and Inclusion in social protection paper which focuses on the key considerations to be taken into account in the design of social protection responses during COVID-19.

UN Women. 2021. *Experiences of Women with Disabilities in the Asia-Pacific Region during COVID-19.* New York: UN Women.

This paper provides results from consultations with women with disabilities from 10 economies across the Asia and Pacific region. It provides recommendations specific to the inclusion of women with disabilities in the response and recovery from the COVID-19 pandemic and beyond. It deals with poverty and economic impacts, health, and sexual and reproductive health rights, lack of information and data, mental health, education, limited mobility and isolation, unpaid care, violence and abuse, and issues for women with disabilities in institutions.

United Nations. 2020. *Policy Brief no. 69: Leaving No One behind: The COVID-19 crisis through the disability and gender lens.* New York: UN Department of Economic and Social Affairs.

A set of recommendations is provided to this policy brief highlights the impact of COVID-19 on women and girls with disabilities and provides policy guidance for governments and other stakeholders to adopt inclusive and accessible measures to not only mitigate the adverse impacts of the crisis but build resilient societies.

8.4   Water Security and Water, Sanitation, and Hygiene

As with other infrastructure sectors addressed in this publication, there is a very little research that looks specifically at women and girls with disabilities in WASH other than accessing menstrual health needs. This is exemplified in a study released in 2021 by the London School of Hygiene and Tropical Medicine which reviewed 16 WASH policies in Cambodia and Bangladesh. The study compared the policies against a framework of 21 human rights concepts deemed essential for universal, equitable, and accessible health services. It found 14% of the reports addressed disability inclusion and 33% gender inclusion. There was little in either section, however, that referred specifically to women with disabilities. Of the 333 references to human rights concepts for persons with disabilities in WASH, 90% looked at persons with disabilities as a broad group with 7% referred specifically to women with disabilities, 4% to adults, generally and 4% to children with disabilities.[118] The need for a dedicated focus addressing women and girls with disabilities in water security remains an area where more research and programming needs to be done.

The World Bank notes the lack of adequate data to assess the number of persons with disabilities facing water scarcity and lack of access noting evidence of the marginalization and invisibility of persons with disabilities in water sector development programs.[119] The UN's 2018 *Disability and Development Report* states persons with disabilities are more likely to live in households without access to adequate WASH, with further likelihood of households with persons with disabilities living in higher levels of poverty.[120]

The need for WASH programs in institutional settings has been highlighted within reports by the Special Rapporteur on the Human Right to Safe Drinking Water and Sanitation.[121] Due to poverty and isolation, some women with disabilities may be homeless or live in slum areas with inadequate WASH facilities. Water points may be inaccessible, or they may experience stigma when attempting access.

People with physical disabilities are more likely to experience accessibility issues in collecting water and WASH. In addition, some cultures believe that persons with disabilities can contaminate water sources and latrines. Persons with disabilities often require a longer time to access water or use latrines and have a higher dependency on others for assistance.

Women and girls with disabilities face additional gender discrimination in accessing amenities, including menstrual hygiene management, appropriate disposal, accessible spaces to wash and dry sanitary products and incinerators, and privacy. A lack of these facilities prevent women and girls with disabilities from accessing schools, workplaces, and public areas. These factors lead to discrimination and stigma based on both gender and disability. Enabling a safe and conducive environment at all levels is required to ensure the needs of women and girls with disabilities are met.

---

[118] N. Scherer et al. 2021. The Inclusion of Rights of People with Disabilities and Women and Girls in Water, Sanitation, and Hygiene Policy Documents and Programs of Bangladesh and Cambodia: Content Analysis Using EquiFrame. *International Journal of Environmental Research and Public Health*. Vol. 18. p. 12.

[119] World Bank. 2017. *Including Persons with Disabilities in Water Sector Operations: A Guidance Note*. Washington, DC: The World Bank.

[120] United Nations. 2018. *Disability and Development Report Realizing the Sustainable Development Goals by, for and with persons with disabilities*. New York: UN Department of Economic and Social Affairs. p. 121.

[121] Centre for Advocacy and Research (CFAR). 2020. *Sexual and Gender Minorities and COVID-19: Guidance for WASH Delivery*. Delhi: CFAR. pp. 3 and 9.

8.4.1 Issues and Barriers for Women and Girls with Disabilities in Water Security

Table 10: Issues and Barriers for Women and Girls with Disabilities in Water Security

Key Issue	Evidence
Women and girls with disabilities face increased health and safety risks due to limited access to water and sanitation hygiene (WASH) facilities.	• Women and girls with disabilities face significant barriers in toileting and independently collecting water for themselves. Often water sources (i.e., wells, taps) are a distance to travel. Women and girls with disabilities risk falling into a well or pond. • Latrines may be inaccessible due to physical disability. Women and girls with disabilities may need to defecate in open areas, which the United Nations (UN) cites as increasing the danger of accidents, rape, and other adverse safety and health issues.[a] • Women and girls with disabilities are more likely to experience urinary incontinence due to obstructions in childbirth, and a lack of sanitation and hygiene in medical care. This increases the need for women with disabilities for safe and accessible WASH facilities (see case study).[b]
Women and girls with disabilities experience specific and differential types of discrimination and exclusion in the water sector.	• The World Bank's *Including Persons with Disabilities in Water Sector Operations* identifies several social, cultural, and attitudinal barriers in the water sector. A traditional role for women is to collect water and manage household water tasks. If women are not able to do this, they may be seen as a burden on families and the community, which impacts on their self-esteem and limits social and community engagement. Misconceptions are also held about women with disabilities' reproductive health and hygiene. Women with disabilities are excluded from consultations on water management. The dependence of persons with disabilities on others increases health risks as well as the potential for sexual and financial exploitation.[c] • Girls with disabilities face a high risk of school dropout due to the inaccessibility of WASH facilities at school.[d]
Using a joint gendered disability inclusion approach directly addresses the specific needs of women and girls with disabilities rather than separate gender and disability approaches.	• A Christian Blind Mission program on gender and disability WASH initially engaged separate gender and disability advisers; however, it found the different approaches created confusion, reinforced a siloed approach of addressing the issues, and presented additional work for staff and partners for a WASH program. The project adopted a gender and disability-inclusive approach and developed strategies to address the underlying cultural and structural issues of inequity.[e]

[a] United Nations 2018. Disability and Development Report Realizing the Sustainable Development Goals by, for and with Persons with Disabilities. New York: UN Department of Economic and Social Affairs, p. 125.

[b] London School of Hygiene and Tropical Medicine. 2020. *Water, Women and Disability Study: Main Report.* Canberra: DFAT.

[c] London School of Hygiene and Tropical Medicine. 2020. *Water, Women and Disability Study: Main Report.* Canberra: DFAT. pp. 18 and 31.

[d] World Bank 2017. *Including Persons with Disabilities in Water Sector Operations: A Guidance Note.* Washington, DC: The World Bank. p. 23.

[e] Water for Women. 2019. *Disability Inclusive Systems Strengthening in WASH: How Can We Do It Better?* Canberra: DFAT.

8.4.2 Potential Opportunities and Entry Points for Programming

• CBM has developed a specific guide on integrating an approach to address issues of gender and disability to "do development" better.[122] It cites the inclusion of working with OPDs as critical from the outset; however, it also noted that OPDs can be gender-blind and inadvertently perpetuate gender inequalities. CBM suggests ensuring that the OPDs are gender-aware, or jointly work with women's organizations. Gender-aware OPDs were used as a partner throughout the project scoping work, delivering training and assisting in the development of local tools. Working with women with disabilities in programming not only increased access to local needs in WASH, but role modelled the capacity and leadership potential of women with disabilities.

---

[122] See additional resources section at the end of this sector guideline for more details.

- The World Bank advocates the use of access and safety audits to identify accessibility and safety concerns for women and girls with disabilities due to the higher safety risks they experience accessing water and sanitation resources. This includes addressing menstrual hygiene management, privacy, disposal bins with lids, accessible spaces to wash and dry sanitary products, and incinerators.[123]

- Water management and WASH data should be disaggregated by sex, age, disability, and ethnicity. Using the WGQs enables a more accurate collection of disability data.

- Training for staff and volunteers is needed to ensure equity of access for the most marginalized women and girls with disabilities. The Centre for Advocacy and Research in India worked with a local transgender NGO to facilitate the installation of accessible water facilities in settlements where transgender people lived. IRC in Pakistan now employs a transgender staff member and transgender people are on the local WASH advisory teams. Likewise, the inclusion of women with disabilities from Indigenous and ethnic groups in WASH teams leads to more effective implementation and increases the employment of diverse women with disabilities.

- With the inclusion of adaptative devices, irrigation systems can be modified for persons with disabilities.[124] Modifications increase the dignity of women and girls with disabilities by enabling them to address their own and their families' WASH needs, as well as provide income for farming and home gardens.

- Water sector programming can build community campaigns into project activities to dispel inaccurate perceptions of women and girls with disabilities. This includes harmful beliefs such as that persons with disabilities contaminate water. Community campaigns can promote the rights of women and girls with disabilities to safe and equitable water services and promote the active role of women with disabilities and diverse groups in community decision-making processes and employment.

- It should not be assumed that women with disabilities do not work in farming or livelihood activities. Women with disabilities have unique insights into waterways, draining and irrigation systems, and can provide information about water sources that are inaccessible to persons with disabilities. Only women with specific types of physical disabilities will be unable to do this work. They can advise regarding the state of latrines and open defecation. As such, it is important to include women with disabilities in community data gathering exercises, especially indigenous women with disabilities, as they have specialized, cultural knowledge regarding water systems and climate adaptive agricultural techniques.

- The United States Agency for International Development (USAID) funded a project specifically training women with disabilities in aquaponics which combines aquaculture with hydroponics, conserving water and space and producing a sustainable supply of fish and fresh produce. This climate-smart and water-efficient initiative not only provided food to women with disabilities and their families in a food-insecure region, but it also provided the women with an ongoing source of income.[125]

[123] World Bank 2017. *Including Persons with Disabilities in Water Sector Operations: A Guidance Note.* Washington, DC: The World Bank. p. 23.

[124] INMED Partnerships for Children. 2020. *INMED's agricultural training empowers disabled women and youth in the Free State.* Website blog.

[125] INMED Partnerships for Children 2020. *INMED's agricultural training empowers disabled women and youth in the Free State.* INMED. https://inmed.org/inmeds-agricultural-training-empowers-disabled-women-and-youth-in-the-free-state/.

- Women with disabilities are capable of highly technical work in water management. Women with neurodiversity, for example, may be exceptional data programmers. The United Kingdom (UK) Government Communications Headquarters states that employing neurodivergent women has led to better pattern recognition, trending, creativity, and innovation.[126]

8.4.3 Sample Indicators for Water Security Programs to Address the Needs of Women and Girls with Disabilities

Table 11: Sample Indicators for Water Security Programs to Address the Needs of Women and Girls with Disabilities

Issue	Indicator
Decision-making, leadership, participation, legal and institutional reform	
Gender-responsive organizations of persons with disabilities (OPDs) or those led by or focused on working with women with disabilities play a significant role in providing key advisory services in water management, especially regarding the unique barriers faced by women and girls with disabilities in water sanitation and hygiene (WASH).	Number of consultations with local OPDs led by or working with women with disabilities throughout the project cycle. Number of focus group discussions held with diverse groups of women with disabilities segregated by type of disability. Number of focus group discussions held with women who are carers of family members with disabilities. Number of project activities that have directly addressed the issues raised by OPDs, local women with disabilities, and women as carers of family members with disabilities.
Increasing the role of women with disabilities throughout all levels of the project cycle in the water sector can lead to gender- and disability-inclusive water practices and recognize the skills of women with disabilities.	Number of women with disabilities in decision-making roles in water-related institutions. Number and type of initiatives to promote women's participation in water-related decision-making and leadership positions. Number of women with disabilities in water user groups noting the number specifically in management or leadership roles. Number of policies or measures approved or supported in implementation in the water sector that address gender and disability inclusion and equal opportunity.
Human development	
The provision of safe and accessible basic WASH facilities improves the health and dignity of women and girls with disabilities, and for their access to school, employment, and public places.	Number of WASH facilities for girls with disabilities installed in schools with accessibility, adequate privacy, space, and resources for menstrual hygiene management. Number and annual percentage of increase of girls with disabilities attending school. Number of health clinics, markets, and communal WASH facilities that are upgraded to universal design with privacy, space, and resources for menstrual hygiene management. Percentage of population accessing safe drinking water disaggregated by age, sex, type of disability, and ethnicity. Percentage of households with a family member with a disability having an accessible sanitation facility that can be used by all family members.
Decreasing time poverty and drudgery	
Access to safe water and WASH relieves the time burden for women with disabilities, as well as for women who are carers of family members with disabilities.	Number of irrigation systems, community water sources (taps or wells) modified for use by women and girls with disabilities in safe locations. Number of women and girls with disabilities who have saved a minimum of 30 minutes as a result of their access to safe water.

continued of next page

---

[126] Jolly and Jasper. 2022. Organisations want to recruit more women with autism, dyslexia and ADHD to work in cybersecurity roles. *The Guardian.* https://www.theguardian.com/society/2022/nov/16/neurodiverse-women-sought-for-jobs-at-gchq-and-bae-systems.

Table 11 continued

Issue	Indicator
Economic empowerment	
The water sector has the potential to employ a higher number of women with disabilities to increase their income and alleviate poverty.	Number of women with disabilities in WASH teams, disaggregated by age, type of disability, and ethnicity. Number and percentage of women with disabilities employed in project tracked annually.
Eliminating harmful social norms and violence against women and girls with disabilities, and increasing resilience	
Reducing harmful social perceptions of women and girls with disabilities places them at less risk of physical, sexual, and financial abuse.	Number and percentage of women and girls with disabilities who report feeling safer accessing water and using community latrines. Number of trainings provided to water specialists, managers, and staff, to implement water resource management practices addressing gender-responsive disability inclusion. Percentage of trainees who self-report increased awareness of gender and disability discriminatory practices in water management and knowledge to integrate gender sensitive and accessible solutions.

Source: Author.

8.4.4   Case Study on Water Sector

> #### Box 16: Water Case Study: Water, Sanitation, and Hygiene for Women with Disabilities in Vanuatu
>
> A large-scale study on water, women, and disability was conducted in northern provinces of Torba and Sanma in Vanuatu from 2018–2022 by World Vision Vanuatu and the International Centre for Evidence in Disability at the London School of Hygiene and Tropical Medicine.
>
> Many women in the study cited significant barriers in accessing latrines due to the distance, unsafe access, poor lighting, no privacy and the lack of disability accommodations inside the latrine.
>
> The report details deeply held cultural norms which perpetuate harmful menstrual beliefs and taboos in various parts of Vanuatu. For example, it is believed that women and girls will kill crops by touch, and due to being unclean they must not touch family food. They must collect their own water for personal use and to wash their reusable menstrual products and use separate latrines and bathing areas. In Torba province, menstrual huts are constructed where local menstruating women must live. One woman stated:
>
> > When a woman menstruates, she mustn't live with her husband because she is sick. She can cause the husband to be sick with asthma, or they might have a pot belly or even get sick with intestinal gas. We women are different to men. This [menstruation] is a disease itself. (Woman, urban, seeing functional limitation.)
>
> *continued of next page*

Box 16 continued

For women and girls with disabilities, living in a hut deprives them of their usual family support, however, some of the participants in the study reflected on the positive aspect of this situation, as expressed below:

> When I get my period…for me, I feel good because when I get my period, I take a break. I take a break from everything, such as cooking, going out…For me, it's like a holiday. (Woman, urban, seeing functional limitation)[a]

When women with disabilities also experience fecal and urinary incontinence, additional issues arise. Without bedpans or commodes, or the ability to buy incontinence products due to cost, they use uncovered buckets next to their beds. One woman in the study talks of relying on her 4-year-old son to collect water, clean feces and urine from the bucket latrine, and make meals, preventing him from attending preschool. She tries to do as much as she can to avoid asking her son. She comments:

> And then he said, "Mama, I'm too tired now." And then he'll sleep without eating. I'll feel sorry for him. "Don't fetch water, just wet the towel at its end and bring it here." …I clean my private parts—I use the towel to wipe from my bum to the front. But I don't wipe my full body because he's tired. (Woman, urban, walking and self-care functional limitations).[b]

[a] World Vision Vanuatu and the International Centre for Evidence in Disability at the London School of Hygiene and Tropical Medicine. 2020. *Water, Women, and Disability Study Main Report*. Canberra: DFAT. p. 47.
[b] World Vision Vanuatu and the International Centre for Evidence in Disability at the London School of Hygiene and Tropical Medicine. 2020. *Water, Women, and Disability Study Main Report*. Canberra: DFAT. p. 48.
Source: Permission granted from Department of Foreign Affairs and Trade as the funder of the publication.

8.4.5   Useful Resources

Water for Women. 2019. *Disability-Inclusive Systems Strengthening in WASH: How Can We Do It Better?* Canberra: DFAT.

The growing commitment to disability inclusive WASH within the sector has seen much progress in terms of accessible WASH infrastructure at all levels and support for people with disabilities to manage their WASH needs within their households and communities. The WASH sector is also increasingly focused on the broader enabling environment for WASH policy and practice, or on strengthening 'WASH systems'. The linkage of these two streams of work, however, remains an area for further learning and innovation. This Learning Brief 'Disability Inclusive Systems Strengthening in WASH: How can we do it better?' reflects on the discussions held during the Systems Strengthening for Inclusive WASH learning event in December 2019 in Nepal.

World Bank. 2017. *Including Persons with Disabilities in Water Sector Operations: A Guidance Note.* Washington, DC: The World Bank.

The note collates recommended strategies and practices in disability-inclusive development programming. It identifies entry points for disability-inclusive water operations in World Bank Group-supported programs, projects and advisory services, and analytics. Case studies, including the World Bank Group and external examples, are provided to highlight the use of recommended practices. In addition, the annexes list several technical assistance resources to support task teams and clients in ensuring that infrastructure and services are inclusive of all persons with disabilities.

Inclusion of Rights of People with Disabilities and Women and Girls in Water, Sanitation, and Hygiene Policy Documents and Programs of Bangladesh and Cambodia: Content Analysis Using EquiFrame. International Journal in Environmental Research and Public Health, 18.

This study examines the extent to which WASH policy documentation in Bangladesh and Cambodia include information on the rights of persons with disabilities, and women and girls, and the degree to which policy commitments have been translated into program implementation. The study separately identifies the rights of persons with disabilities and the rights of women and girls in WASH policy documents of Bangladesh and Cambodia. It then studies how the rights of persons with disabilities and women and girls have been addressed in programming. The study found more references to women as a whole of population group (33%) than for persons with disabilities as a whole (14%); however, there was little attention to women and girls with disabilities as a distinct group. It notes accessibility as a core issue, but little reference was made to empowerment, family support, and sustainable service provision. It also found that the rights enshrined in documents were not evident in programming.

Water Aid. 2017. *Gender Equality and Disability Inclusion within Water, Sanitation and Hygiene Exploring Integrated Approaches to Addressing Inequality.* Melbourne: WaterAid.

To ensure universal access, the document takes a rights-based approach to WASH, addressing equality and nondiscrimination with an approach based on participation and inclusion. The paper poses and answers two main questions: how can the WASH sector continue to improve practice on gender and disability, and how can an integrated approach to the two intersectional issues of gender and disability help us "do development" better?

8.5   Transport

There is significant research and programming that has focused on the specific needs of women in transport. This includes issues of safety; lighting; accounting for the cost and availability of short and frequent trips to school, health facilities, and markets; and the use of feeder roads rather than main streets and highways. There has also been significant work on addressing the needs of persons with disabilities in transportation, including accessibility and universal design standards for those with physical and sensory disabilities (i.e., sight and hearing). However, transport systems rarely consider the needs of people with cognitive impairments (i.e., developmental delays, difficulties with information processing and memory) who tend to avoid public transport, especially at busy times.

They are often not able to safely and securely navigate on their own and are often focused on personal security (i.e., harassment or crime) and safety (i.e., avoiding physical danger or harm). Women with cognitive impairments face higher levels of harassment and abuse on transportation.[127]

There is very little research or programming that looks specifically at the multiple and differential needs of women and girls with disabilities in transportation. Women and girls with disabilities are more likely to suffer higher levels of poverty and less able to afford their choice of transportation. Barriers to transport access, gender inequality, and disability stigma and discrimination lead to decreased access to education and health services.

There is no global data on the usage of transportation by women with disabilities. However, the United Nations *Disability and Development Report* indicates more than 30% of persons with disabilities in some countries find transportation is not accessible.[128] While this information is not sex disaggregated, the issues identified below indicate women and girls with disabilities travel less than men due to additional attitudinal and safety issues. In contrast, a 2020 study on inclusive mobility found women as caregivers made almost 50% more trips than men and non-caregivers due to more complex routes and trip chains and a wider need for travel.[129] This represents another gender issue impacting heavily on women's lives and time burden due to the social norm that the mother is the primary carer of family members with disabilities.

A European Commission study refers to transport systems being "typically designed for an idealized group of middle-class, adult, self-empowered users who have no major mental, sensory, or physical disabilities and who are uninhibited about navigating the transport system by themselves."[130] Analysis of data from this study shows that the most complex and greatest unmet needs in transport are for women with disabilities, children, and caregivers.

Women and girls with disabilities experience many of the same barriers to transport access as men with disabilities, along with many additional issues. Some of these barriers affect all women and girls with disabilities, and some are specific to culture, religion, and local context. Universal design is essential for physical and sensory accessibility and includes ramps, elevators, ticketing desks, and machines at a height for persons with disabilities, adequate lighting, wheelchair accessible toilets, audio and braille instructions, as well as individual access to wheelchairs, white canes, and hearing aids.

---

[127] K. Tovaas. 2020. *How to Make Inclusive Mobility a Reality: 8 Principles and Tools for a Fair(er) Transport System*. Brussels: European Commission. pp. 27–29.

[128] United Nations. 2018. *Disability and Development Report Realizing the Sustainable Development Goals by, for and with Persons with Disabilities*. New York: UN Department of Economic and Social Affairs. p. 14.

[129] K. Tovaas. 2020. *How to Make Inclusive Mobility a Reality: 8 Principles and Tools for a Fair(er) Transport System*. Brussels: European Commission, p. 13.

[130] K. Tovaas. 2020. *How to Make Inclusive Mobility a Reality: 8 Principles and Tools for a Fair(er) Transport System*. Brussels: European Commission. p. 6.

8.5.1   Issues and Barriers for Women and Girls with Disabilities in Transport

Table 12: Issues and Barriers for Women and Girls with Disabilities in Transport

Key Issues	Evidence
Women and girls with disabilities face prejudice from transport service providers due to the combination of gender and disability discrimination.	• In a review of poverty and sustainable transport, several studies found that private operators will try to avoid or discourage persons with disabilities from travelling on free or concessionary tickets as they are not compensated for these discounts. Although this occurs for all persons with disabilities, the issue is particularly acute for women and girls with disabilities and leads to increased safety concerns.[a] • Transportation systems often only address physical and some sensory (hearing and sight) impairments, with cognitive and psychosocial disabilities being invisible. Women with invisible forms of disability are less likely to voice their needs due to social norms and embarrassment to claim what is seen to be "special treatment" or an inconvenience to others. Barriers for women and girls with psychosocial and cognitive disabilities include crowded spaces, bright lighting, noise, and fast, brisk instructions. Women and girls with cognitive and psychosocial disabilities find it harder to look people in the eyes when instructions are given. This is often misinterpreted as being rude and dismissive and can result in abuse from service staff. Alternatively, service staff may only speak to the carer or the accompanying adult assuming women and girls with disabilities are "infantile" or unable to understand.[b]
The impact of inaccessible transport for women and girls with disabilities leads to less access to basic and essential services.	• A study of the "invisible" needs of women with disabilities in Malaysia found that for many women with disabilities to be able to attend accessible education, training, or employment, they needed to live a long distance from their family. Without accessible transport, their contact with family members and friends was difficult, lessening their support system, and leading to or exacerbating psychological issues.[c] • Inaccessible public transport is an obstacle to accessing health clinics for women and girls with disabilities, especially those with sensory, mobility, and cognitive impairments. • Women with disabilities in many countries use motorcycle taxis due their availability, door-to-door travel, and freedom from harassment. However, the cost of motorcycle taxis is a barrier for people experiencing poverty (including many women with disabilities), who only use them for emergency transport and make major efforts to meet the costs.
Women and girls with disabilities, and people of diverse sexual orientation, gender identity, gender expression, and sex characteristics (SOGIESC) face increased prejudice and discrimination from the general public on transportation.	• People of diverse SOGIESC face hate crimes and higher levels of perceived unsafety on transport compared to the general population, and this increases for those with disabilities. Research suggests more than two-thirds of the community are unlikely to disclose their sexual orientation through behavior or dress on public transport and are likely to restrict their use of public transport during times of perceived unsafety.[d] • A Malaysian study identified the targeting of women with disabilities by men due to "perceived vulnerability, threats, the presumption of impunity and prejudices against disabled women." Offenders see women with disabilities as "vulnerable" victims and assume they will not file complaints (note c). • A UN Women study on safe transport for women and girls in Port Moresby, Papua New Guinea found 84% of 160 survey respondents (124 female, 36 male) believed public transport services were not suitable for persons with disabilities. Women with disabilities had the least access to transport, linked to both poverty and accessibility, and when they did use public transport, they experienced high levels of harassment and violence. Many women with disabilities travelled outside of busy times to avoid being assaulted, limiting their access to regular employment.[e]

continued of next page

Table 12 continued

Key Issues	Evidence
Women and girls with disabilities are underrepresented in all aspects of transport decision-making and lack equality of access to employment in the sector.	• Women and persons with disabilities are both underrepresented in accessing labor in transport construction; however, quotas have often been included for both of these groups. Very few of these quotas are filled in reality, even when mandated by the government; disability quotas are generally filled by men, while gender quotas are filled by women without disabilities. • An Asian Development Bank (ADB) study found that women and persons with disabilities are disadvantaged in accessing manual work in the road construction sector. This work is seen as "heavy," although the study notes that "heavy" and "light" work are often identified by cultural norms of work rather than the physical effort required. This makes it doubly hard for women with disabilities to access construction work, despite many jobs not requiring physical strength and many forms of disability not being physical. The report also cites poor safety and security, and unsafe labor camps (which should not be an acceptable standard for any workers).[f] • Women are underrepresented in most areas of the transportation sector, especially senior roles. When women have a disability, their representation in all aspects of the paid workforce drop significantly. The World Bank's project experience notes the inclusion of women in stakeholder consultations for transport planning often leads to transport design with better access and safety for other vulnerable users such as persons with disabilities, children, and the older people.[g] Following from this, the direct inclusion of women with disabilities, drawing from their expert knowledge and lived experience, would provide even better planning for the needs of women and girls with disabilities who are possibly the most vulnerable transport users (especially those who are poor, elderly, Indigenous, from ethnic groups, and illiterate).

[a] P. Starkey and J. Hine. 2014. Poverty and sustainable transport: How transport affects poor people with policy implications for poverty reduction. Nairobi: UN-Habitat and the Overseas Development Institute. p. 45.

[b] OECD. 2009. *Cognitive Impairment, Mental Health and Transport: Design with Everyone in Mind*. Paris: OECD and International Transport Forum.

[c] A. Iudici, L. Bertoli, and E. Faccio. 2017. The "invisible" needs of women with disabilities in transportation systems. *Crime Prevention and Community Safety*. September. pp. 264–275.

[d] K. Tovaas. 2020. *How to Make Inclusive Mobility a Reality: 8 Principles and Tools for a Fair(er) Transport System*. Brussels: European Commission. p. 13.

[e] UN Women. 2014. Ensuring Safe Transport with and For Women and Girls in Port Moresby. Papua New Guinea: UN Women. p. 26

[f] ADB. 2020. *Gender Equality and Social Inclusion Diagnostic of Selected Sectors in Nepal*. Manila: ADB. p. 75.

[g] World Bank. 2010. *Mainstreaming Gender in Road Transport: Operational Guidance for World Bank Staff*. Washington, DC: World Bank. p. 10.

8.5.2 Potential Opportunities and Entry Points for Programming

• Consultation with OPDs led by women or working with women's groups should be a key source of consultation at the outset of any planning. The technical expertise of women with disabilities should be drawn from to identify their specific needs in the transport sector. These groups can facilitate focus groups of local women and girls with disabilities, as well as men and people of diverse SOGIESC to develop a stakeholder analysis of barriers in local transport systems. This should include a diversity of women with disabilities (including very poor people, Indigenous or ethnic groups, the illiterate and those that do not speak the majority language who do not have access to services). Additionally, women with various physical, sensory, cognitive, and psychosocial disabilities should be included (in separate groups with appropriate accommodations provided by female service providers, if possible). OPDs can often provide these services; however, it should be noted that OPDs, especially those run by and for women receive very little funding and often rely on volunteer labor. To value and respect the provision of specialist technical knowledge, OPDs and women with disabilities should have their expertise recognized, valued, and paid appropriately.

- Include diverse groups of women with disabilities, as well as women who are the primary carers of family members with disabilities in local stakeholder analysis, transport surveys, household surveys, and detailed activity analysis at the household level. Including feedback from women and girls with disabilities in the monitoring and evaluation of public transport can be conducted during the design and implementation of activities to help to understand what the transport system constraints are for women and girls with disabilities, including travel needs, user patterns, concerns, priorities, time pressures, preferences, required accommodations, and personal safety.

- Conduct a baseline study to assess transport usage and satisfaction ratings of diverse women with disabilities and underrepresented groups. This could be contracted to an OPD led by women or working with women with disabilities. This could be followed up with the same OPD on an annual basis over the period of the projects.

- Ensure all information systems collect SADD.

- Provide key roles for women with disabilities in the transport sector, including as liaison staff for women and girls with disabilities, members of core staff, project and advisory teams (including paid advisor roles), and members of user committees. Women with disabilities can also be provided with priority and reduced rate spaces for entrepreneurial activities at transport hubs close to women's disability toilets and security.

- Universal design implemented by transport construction contractors must be informed by local guidance as outlined above. In addition, an assessment should be undertaken by male and female persons with disabilities to ensure quality standards are upheld.

- Increased access to transportation for women with disabilities needs to include universal and gender-responsive design principles, as well as an understanding of and awareness of how to use new systems, such as ticketing booths for diverse disabilities. Women and girls with disabilities are less likely to ask for special assistance or accommodations or may not know they exist in transport services. When new services incorporate disability access women and girls with disabilities may not be aware of these or how to use them. Awareness sessions could be held for groups of women with disabilities once new transportation systems have been completed so they can become familiar with the new system. This can be conducted prior to the official opening when the stations are quiet.

- To address barriers for women and girls with disabilities to access school and health services, local and culturally appropriate services that could be provided include special buses to collect girls with disabilities, and adaptations to vehicles for girls with disabilities to have a safe space at the front of vehicles to increase access, reduce discrimination, and provide safety. Access to health centers could include dedicated free or reduced fare buses, taxis, or public motor vehicles (PMVs). Many countries have female taxi drivers and PMV drivers. Women transport providers could be trained in understanding the needs of women with disabilities with their services promoted by health centers and OPDs. These door-to-door services for women with disabilities could be developed as a model to offer a secure transport service for women (especially for those travelling at night) and to create more jobs for women. Reduced rates could be offered for transport to essential services.[131]

---

[131]   K. Tovaas. 2020. *How to Make Inclusive Mobility a Reality: 8 Principles and Tools for a Fair(er) Transport System.* Brussels: European Commission. p. 50.

- To address the harassment of women with disabilities on vehicles and at transport hubs, women only areas can be created. These are common in South Asia and need to be made accessible for women with disabilities. Providing quiet, safe, and secure spaces away from congested areas would benefit women and girls with cognitive disabilities.

- Training is required for transportation staff (including planners and service staff) to increase awareness of the needs and concerns of women and girls with disabilities, and the diversity of their disabilities. There is also a need to address the gender and disability discrimination women with disabilities face from transportation staff, as well as other transport users. This requires dedicated training programs for transportation staff, as well as awareness campaigns for transport users which could include posters, voice announcements, and digital campaigns.

8.5.3 Sample Indicators for Transportation Systems to Address the Needs of Women and Girls with Disabilities

Table 13: Sample Indicators for Transportation Systems to Address the Needs of Women and Girls with Disabilities

Issue	Indicator
Decision-making, leadership, participation, legal and institutional reform	
Including women with disabilities as advisors in project design will ensure transport programming addresses the needs of persons with disabilities.	Number of women with disabilities on project and advisory teams/paid advisor roles.
Directly consulting with local organizations of persons with disabilities (OPDs) led by or working with women with disabilities in the process of project design will provide useful guidance for effective interventions.	Number of specific initiatives in the project drawn from consultations with local OPDs led by or working with women with disabilities Number of specific initiatives in the project drawn from focus group discussions held with local diverse groups of women with disabilities.
Human development	
The increase in safe and accessible transport for women and girls with disabilities can increase their attendance at health clinics.	Number and percentage of increase of women and girls with disabilities attending health clinics.
The increase in safe and accessible transport for women and girls with disabilities can increase the school attendance rate for girls with disabilities.	Number of initiatives addressing women and girls with disabilities' access to education. Number and percentage of increase of women and girls with disabilities attending school.
When women with disabilities are aware of, and can use, transport accommodations their travel rates can improve.	Number of initiatives and/or communication campaigns addressing gender-responsive universal design and reasonable accommodations that are incorporated into transport programming.

continued of next page

Table 13 continued

Issue	Indicator
Decreasing time poverty and drudgery	
Conducting a baseline study or updated assessment will identify changes in transport usage and satisfaction ratings. This could be contracted to a OPD led by women or working with women with disabilities.	Baseline study results of women with disabilities user patterns in transport and satisfaction ratings. Baseline study results of women carers of family members with disabilities in user patterns in transport and satisfaction ratings.
The same OPD could be used to track changes in usage and satisfaction over the period of the project.	Number of women with disabilities reporting increased usage of transport facilities and/or satisfaction with transport usage.
Economic empowerment	
The transport sector has the potential to employ a higher number of skilled and unskilled women with disabilities to increase their income and alleviate poverty.	Percentage of women with disabilities employed in all levels of transport employment and high-level decision-making. Percentage of women with disabilities within mandatory quotas for the employment of women in skilled and unskilled positions. Percentage of women with disabilities in mandatory quotas for the employment of persons with disabilities. Number of women with disabilities employed at transport hubs as service staff and liaison personnel for persons with disabilities. Annual % increases of women with disabilities employed over life of the project in skilled and unskilled positions.
Livelihood and entrepreneurial opportunities connected to transport services can provide income for women with disabilities.	Number of initiatives for entrepreneurial income for women with disabilities connected to transport systems. Number of women with disabilities receiving new income source. Percentage of increase of income annually.
Eliminating harmful social norms and violence against women and girls with disabilities, and increasing resilience	
Increasing accessible, safe, and harassment-free urban facilities will increase the real and perceived safety for women and girls with disabilities at transit centers.	Number of women's disability toilets with adequate space for menstrual hygiene and changing a catheter. Number of disability-friendly priority women's spaces with adequate lighting and security for women with disabilities to wait for transport and on buses/trains (these could include separate queues, carriages, panic buttons, and others). Number of initiatives that are designed specifically to create safe and accessible transportation for women and girls with disabilities.
Increased understanding of the issues faced by women and girls with disabilities can lead to behavior change of transport operators and the public.	Number of training sessions for transportation staff on the rights of women with disabilities and strategies to address discrimination and stigma, including awareness of gender-responsive accommodations for physical, sensory, and cognitive disabilities. Number of initiatives that incorporate accommodations for women and girls with cognitive disabilities into transport design.

Source: Author.

8.5.4 Case Study on Transport

Box 17: Transport Case Study: Trans Peshawar Bus Transport System Peshawar, Pakistan

The Asian Development Bank (ADB), with Agence Française de Développement, the Government of Khyber Pakhtunkhwa, Pak Everbright Development Organization (PEDO), and Peshawar Development Authority worked with TransPeshawar to develop an accessible and inclusive public transport system in Peshawar, Pakistan.

The involvement of the locally based Peshawar organization of persons with disabilities, PEDO, was a critical aspect of planning from the outset to address the specific needs of local persons with disabilities with different types of impairments. Having been established in 2009 by local persons with disabilities, PEDO drew from over a decade of local knowledge and networks to conduct surveys, workshops, consultations, and public meetings with diverse groups of persons with disabilities. PEDO's chief executive officer (CEO) Shahab Ud Din ensured separate discussions were held with women and men with disabilities, with transwomen included in the women's groups. The issues raised by women with disabilities were significant to their usage of public transport and may not have been apparent if they had not been consulted in a space of their own.

Poverty, lack of knowledge, and inability to advocate and travel to services may mean some women in Peshawar may not have access to appropriate accommodations. For instance, local women with disabilities may not have access to wheelchairs and, thus, crawl to access transport. Women with disabilities in Peshawar generally only have access to orthopedic wheelchairs for general living along with those provided at transportation hubs. These are not appropriate for many women with disabilities as they are designed for the male physique and require modified cushions for pressure relief for the female biology. Many women with disabilities also do not have the physical strength to move the footpads to access transport or elevators, with women leaving their wheelchairs at the station and crawling to use transportation services. However, due to their different size and muscular strength, many women with disabilities may still not be able to access elevators.

Ud Din also stressed the need to address local attitudinal barriers as women and girls only make up 2% of public transport users. Women reported being continuously harassed and made uncomfortable. Their disabilities often meant they could not physically access the prescribed separate rooms or spaces for women on buses or trains. They sometimes need to use the seats in the male sections which leads to harassment and verbal or physical abuse. This is escalated when women with disabilities may not be able to ensure their *hijab* constantly covers their head. Ud Din emphasized that transwomen with disabilities experience additional harassment, such as having abusive slurs shouted at them.

The implementation of the 1981 ordinance in Pakistan for a 2% allocated quota in employment for persons with disabilities has not been adhered to in the transportation sector. Ud Din believes transport hubs for women with disabilities would be a huge benefit, assisting access as well as providing role models for other women in the transport sector.

continued of next page

Box 17 continued

It was critical the Zu Peshawar design drew from Ud Din's organization of persons with disabilities' decades of experience, technical knowledge, and the networks of female staff to consult with local women with disabilities. He suggests various accommodations to support women with disabilities to use public transport including modified wheelchairs, access to women's spaces, and male and female wheelchair-accessible toilets with adequate access to menstrual hygiene and space to change a catheter. He states the provision of two or three daily buses of a different color could be allocated for women with disabilities, as many buses are currently sitting unused at depots. Training and awareness can be provided by organizations, such as PEDO, to address stigma and harassment, noting organizations of persons with disabilities need to be paid for their technical expertise.

Source: Shahab Ud Din, PEDO CEO was interviewed for these guidelines on 22 December 2022. He provided permission for use of this text.

8.5.5   Useful Resources

Iudici, A., Bertoli, L., and Faccio, E. 2017. The "invisible" needs of women with disabilities in transportation systems. *Crime Prevention and Community Safety. September. pp. 264–275.*

This study focuses on the experiences of women with physical disabilities in gaining access to public transportation in Malaysia. The study collected data from in-depth interviews with 33 Malaysian women with physical impairments from low-income and rural families with limited access to transportation. The findings showed many women had experienced significant barriers to accessing public transport, including inaccessibility of public transport and negative attitudes of public transport providers. Their marginalization lessened their access to broader economic and social participation. Women with disabilities also claimed discrimination in public transport services is a significant obstacle for them to live their daily lives.

Starkey, P., and Hine, J. 2014. *Poverty and Sustainable Transport: How Transport Affects Poor People with Policy Implications for Poverty Reduction.* Nairobi: UN-Habitat and the Overseas Development Institute (ODI).

Although this paper does not consider the issues for women and persons with disabilities separately, it considers rural roads in respect to poverty, access and isolation, agricultural production, access to health care and education, non-equal benefits, long-term benefits and negative consequences, policy implications, measurability of pro-poor benefits and investment priorities, and involving rural people in road construction and maintenance. As rural women and girls with disabilities are often poor, with many living in rural areas, these issues are critical for addressing their needs. The paper also notes women and girls with disabilities prefer to use public transport at off-peak times when they are safer; however, there are fewer services available.

Tovaas, K. 2020. *How to Make Inclusive Mobility a Reality: 8 Principles and Tools for a Fair(er) Transport System.* Brussels: European Commission.

This paper looks at the mobility situation for user groups, including older people, children, students, women and caregivers, physically or sensory disabled, and cognitively impaired people, migrants, job seekers, people in rural areas, those without a driver's license, and people with a low income. These user groups have varying needs in terms of accessibility, affordability, convenience, efficiency, empowerment, empathy, gender equity, and safety. The resource provides recommendations on how to make mobility more inclusive, accessible, and fair. Furthermore, it evaluates experiences, lessons learned, and viable business models, to improve the social dimension of sustainable transport. Women's safety and equitable access to transport are still the primary barriers for women's mobility, with direct impacts on their participation in economic, social, and political opportunities. Women also make more multiple-trip chains using public transport and are still the primarily responsible for caring for children or elderly relatives.

UN Women. 2014. *Ensuring Safe Transport with and for Women and Girls in Port Moresby.* Papua New Guinea: UN Women.

The report reflects the results of the Safe Cities Global Initiative for Port Moresby through a scoping study on women's experiences and perceptions of violence in the use of public transport, especially for market vendors, students, and professionals in selected locations across the city. Although focused primarily as a resource for the safety of women and girls in general, the resource also addresses some issues for women and girls with disabilities, identifying their challenges in public transport which limits their access to health, education, and employment. Despite frequent experiences of violence, women and girls with disabilities still relied on both PMVs and taxis, as they are least likely to have access to other forms of transportation.

8.6   Urban Development

The New Urban Agenda[132] stresses the specific barriers faced by women and girls, as well as people with disabilities and how their needs are exacerbated when they are living with HIV, older persons, indigenous peoples, slum and informal settlement dwellers, homeless people, smallholder farmers and fishers, refugees and returnees, internally displaced persons and migrants. It calls for data to be disaggregated by income, sex, age, race, ethnicity, migration status, disability, and geographic location.[133]

Gender discrimination leads to many challenges for women in urban areas. Distances between essential services such as schools, health centers, and markets may require trip chaining, resulting in multiple short trips on various, and often overcrowded vehicles. Women report being at risk of and experiencing violence and sexual harassment in public spaces and on public transport. Socially marginalized women lack access to land ownership, adequate housing, electricity, water, and safe public toilets which are well lit and accommodate menstrual hygiene. Over the past several decades increasing attention has been paid to gender issues in urban planning and design. Similarly, widespread attention and universal design principles have improved persons with disabilities' access in city areas

---

[132]   Adopted at the UN Conference on Housing and Sustainable Urban Development (Habitat III) in 2016.
[133]   United Nations. 2016. *New Urban Agenda.* New York: Habitat III Secretariat. paras. 20 and 104.

and, to a lesser extent, people with sensory disabilities such as sight and hearing disabilities. However, very little focus has been placed on addressing the needs and barriers faced by people with cognitive and psychosocial disabilities in urban environments.

Consistent with the other infrastructure sector guidelines (as well as social protection and education), gender and disability inclusion have been addressed as two separate and distinct areas of focus in urban planning. Very few resources or case studies are available that look at the distinct differences, needs, and opportunities for women and girls with disabilities in urban design and planning. Due to the multiple barriers facing women and girls with disabilities in urban areas, there is a need to dedicate more research and partner with women-led focused OPDs to address the needs of some of the most marginalized members of the city.

The *ADB Strategy 2030 Achieving a Prosperous, Inclusive, Resilient, and Sustainable Asia and the Pacific* estimates that 55% of the global population will be living in urban areas by 2030. The Strategy acknowledges urbanization is becoming more complex to manage in the Asia and Pacific region with "making cities more livable" being one of the seven operational priorities. The Strategy notes the need for age, gender, and disability-friendly infrastructure.[134]

8.6.1 Issues and Barriers for Women and Girls with Disabilities in Urban Development

Table 14: Issues and Barriers for Women and Girls with Disabilities in Urban Development

Key Issue	Evidence
Urban planning does not account for the specific needs of women and girls with disabilities.	• The *World Bank Handbook for Gender-Inclusive Urban Planning and Design* states that "in general, cities work better for heterosexual, able-bodied, cisgender men than they do for women, girls, sexual and gender minorities, and people with disabilities."[a] It states that the disadvantages faced by these groups, which includes diverse groups of women with disabilities, in the built environment is not sufficiently understood or accepted by many urban planners. Their lack of responsiveness perpetuates inequality (note a). • The Asian Development Bank (ADB) 2020 publication, *Gender Equality and Social Inclusion Diagnostic of Selected Sectors in Nepal,* identifies that the design of urban areas and services do not reflect gender and social differentiated needs with limited interventions that address discriminatory gender and social norms.[b] Additionally, ADB's 2022 *Inclusive Cities Urban Area Guidelines* identifies that planning for gender-sensitive infrastructure is closely linked to the safety and security of public, residential, and recreational spaces. Inadequate planning and design can increase the risk of violence, leading to gender isolation and discrimination.[c]
Workplace designs, especially in areas where women with disabilities are most likely to work, generally lack adequate accommodations for their needs.	• It is difficult for women with disabilities and the women who are their primary carers to access secure employment. They tend to work in informal sectors with no income security and focus in areas such as handicrafts or market vending, which is time-consuming and poorly paid. For those able to produce and sell in local markets, the spaces may not be easily accessible. Wet markets create additional risks for people with physical disabilities. Accessible female toilets with menstrual hygiene facilities are rarely available and carrying goods to and from markets or vending spaces is not possible for many women with disabilities who are then more likely to pass their goods on to contractors or "middlemen," which decreases their income further.

continued of next page

---

[134]   ADB. 2018. *Strategy 2030: Achieving a Prosperous, Inclusive, Resilient, and Sustainable Asia and the Pacific.* Manila: ADB. p. 15.

Table 14 continued

Key Issue	Evidence
Urban design requires transportation and water, sanitation, and hygiene (WASH) systems to account for the specific needs of women and girls with disabilities, especially those in poverty.	• Women and girls with disabilities face barriers in transportation that is not accessible, safe, frequent, or affordable (see section 8.5 Transport Sector Guidelines). Public transport is often overcrowded and women and girls with disabilities report experiencing stigma, abuse, and violence. This limits the access of women and girls with disabilities, and women who are the primary carers of family members, to schools, health centers, markets, and other public places. • Women and girls with disabilities lose time and experience stress when negotiating access to inadequate potable water and toilets, and face harassment and sexual assault (see section 8.4 Water Security Sector Guidelines). For women who are carers of family members with disabilities, unsafe water adds to the burden of time, compromised health, and limits their ability to bring income into the family. • Due to increased rates of poverty, women with disabilities are more likely to live in small dwellings, informal settlements, or slums often without electricity or adequate WASH facilities, with women generally responsible for household waste disposal. Mosquitoes, flies, and disease are prevalent and place people's health at greater risk.[d]
Disaster preparedness needs to address gendered disability inclusion.	• On average, disasters kill and injure more women than men. Injuries increase the prevalence of women living with a disability.[e] For women and girls with disabilities, disaster preparedness and early warning systems are essential. Women and girls with disabilities, and the women who are their primary carers are less able to evacuate. Evacuation centers may lack access and place people at greater risk due to overcrowding and poor WASH facilities.

[a] World Bank. 2020. *World Bank Handbook for Gender-Inclusive Urban Planning and Design*. Washington, DC: World Bank. p. 8.

[b] ADB. 2022. *Gender Equality and Social Inclusion Diagnostic of Selected Sectors in Nepal October 2020*. Manila: ADB. p. 85.

[c] ADB. 2022. *Inclusive Cities Urban Area Guidelines*. Manila: ADB. p.1.

[d] UN Habitat. 2012. *Gender Issue Guide Urban Planning and Design*. Nairobi: UN Habitat. pp. 17–18.

[e] World Bank. 2020. *World Bank Handbook for Gender-Inclusive Urban Planning and Design*. Washington, DC: World Bank. p. 43.

8.6.2 Potential Opportunities and Entry Points for Programming

(i) Undertaking research on gender- and disability-specific issues in local urban contexts is essential to ensure the most disadvantaged groups of diverse women and girls with disabilities can access basic services in line with their human rights. Supporting research by or in partnership with OPDs led by or working with diverse groups of women and girls with disabilities would provide a solid evidence base for smart urban interventions to meet their needs, as well as profile the active role they can play as productive members of society.[135]

(ii) Women and girls with disabilities are invisible within urban planning and design within local government structures and decision-making. This can be addressed by engaging city planners to work with gender-focused OPDs as clients. This could lead to innovative and climate smart designs that benefit the whole community.

(iii) Local community consultations with women with diverse disabilities is particularly important in poor, urban, and slum areas where women with disabilities live at the margins of society. Ensuring separate stakeholder consultations with these women with disabilities is important to ensure they are comfortable to raise issues they may be embarrassed to raise with other community members. Sessions will provide much richer discussion when they are facilitated by women with disabilities from similar ethnic groups.

---

[135] UN Habitat. 2022. *Cities for Girls Cities for All*. Nairobi: Habitat. p. 17.

(iv) Accessibility for women at markets can be improved through universal design standards (i.e., ramps, pathways, lighting, and the provision of space for women with disabilities near accessible water sources, and toilets with adequate menstrual facilitates). Accessible and safe transportation is needed to assist women with disabilities to move their products to and from the market, minimizing trip chaining, multiple stops, and overcrowded vehicles.

(v)   New smart information systems for urban development have the potential to provide employment opportunities for many women with disabilities. Some computer programming organizations have targeted employing neurodivergent women due to their abilities in pattern recognition, trending, creativity, and innovation.[136] Digital services and markets have potential in urban development to benefit many women with disabilities. However, women with disabilities living in rural areas and who are poor, illiterate, elderly, or do not have access to computers, phones, or internet services will not gain from the digital revolution. Investment in both infrastructure and the on-ground capacity development of skills to use technology is a requirement of LMICs throughout the Asia and Pacific region.

8.6.3 Sample Indicators for Urban Planning to Address the Needs of Women and Girls with Disabilities

Table 15: Sample Indicators for Urban Planning to Address the Needs of Women and Girls with Disabilities

Issue	Indicator
Decision-making, leadership, participation, legal and institutional reform	
Increasing the role of women with disabilities in urban planning and infrastructure can lead to an increase in the responsiveness of urban planning to their specific needs.	Number of policies and strategies that address barriers for women and girls with disabilities in urban planning. Number of modifications in housing design, location and land use planning, or zoning due to consultation with women with disabilities and gender-responsive organizations of persons with disabilities (OPDs). Number and percentage of women vendors with disabilities participating in vendor associations and market management committees. Number of women vendors with disabilities trained in market management skills.
Human development	
Creating affordable and durable housing designed to respond to the needs of households with family members with disabilities improves the living standards for women with disabilities and their families with members with disabilities.	Number of new houses built or upgraded with accommodations for women with disabilities and families with members with disabilities. Number and percentage of women with disabilities who benefit from improved urban infrastructure and services. Number and percentage of loans provided to women with disabilities for housing, water, sanitation, electricity connections, or other improvements. Number of financial institutions with specific finance packages for women with disabilities from informal settlements and low-income areas.

continued of next page

---

[136] J. Jolly. 2022. *Organisations want to recruit more women with autism, dyslexia and ADHD to work in cybersecurity roles. The Guardian.* https://www.theguardian.com/society/2022/nov/16/neurodiverse-women-sought-for-jobs-at-gchq-and-bae-systems (accessed 17 November 2022).

Table 15 continued

Issue	Indicator
Ensuring access to safe water, sanitation, waste disposal, and electricity facilities for households with family members with disabilities in low-income areas will improve the health, safety, and well-being of these families.	Number of households with persons with disabilities gaining access to safe water supplies and electricity connections. Number and percentage of households with persons with disabilities provided with free or subsidized connections to water or electricity, flexible payment arrangements, or lifeline tariffs. Number of households with persons with disabilities with improved sanitation services such as garbage collection, water treatment, sewer networks or households connected to networks. Number of service providers, contractors, and other stakeholders trained on gendered disability exclusion and the needs of diverse women with diverse disabilities.
Decreasing time poverty and drudgery	
Provision of affordable childcare and respite for women with disabilities and carers of family members with disabilities will decrease time poverty for women with disabilities and women as carers for family members with disabilities.	Number of completed infrastructure services that saved at least 30 minutes of time for women and girls with disabilities. Number of health services that cater or are designed for women and girls with disabilities. Number of carers of persons with disabilities trained on appropriate care. Number of community facilities/infrastructure responsive to the needs of women with disabilities. Percentage of affordable childcare services that meet minimum standards of safety and care. Number of women with disabilities using childcare.
Economic empowerment	
The urban development sector has the potential to employ a higher number of women with disabilities to increase their income and alleviate poverty.	Number and percentage of women with disabilities employed during construction according to skilled and unskilled roles. Number of increase in the number of women with disabilities employed in service delivery (e.g., drainage clearance and maintenance, solid waste management, maintenance of toilet blocks, meter reading, water quality testing, maintenance and operations, public hygiene, bill collecting).
Increasing access to credit, providing accommodations in business registration, ensuring universal design in infrastructure and prioritizing vendor spaces for women with disabilities will increase their opportunities in entrepreneurship.	Number and percentage of new businesses established by women with disabilities due to program activities (e.g., expansion of markets, green industries, reforming business registration, increased access to credit, changes to bus routes and timetables). Number of markets upgraded through universal design with reasonable accommodations, including private, clean, and safe sanitation for women vendors and buyers with disabilities. Number of women vendors with disabilities consulted on infrastructure upgrades and reforms. Number of shops or spaces allotted for women vendors with disabilities that are safe, accessible, and close to water, sanitation and hygiene facilities.
Eliminating harmful social norms, violence against women and girls with disabilities, and increasing resilience	
Improved gender and disability-inclusive urban design will increase and has the potential to prevent gender-based violence (GBV).	Number of established networks or groups of women with disabilities, for support and/or platform to report incidences of GBV. Number of public facilities with separate toilets and places modified to meet the needs identified by women and girls with disabilities (e.g., public toilets, community centers, emergency shelters, municipal offices, bus and train stations, public markets). Number of initiatives that address safety risks and increase convenience and access for women and girls with disabilities as transport users. Percentage of women with disabilities who report satisfaction with new or improved infrastructure, facilities, or services.

Source: These indicators draw from the section on urban development from Asian Development Bank. 2013. *Tool Kit on Gender Equality Results and Indicators*. Manila: ADB.

8.6.4 Case Study on Urban Development

Box 18: Case Study of Urban Planning in Georgia Fair Shared Green and Recreational Spaces Guidelines for Gender-Responsive and Inclusive Design

The fair shared green and recreational spaces guidelines for gender-responsive and inclusive design were developed with assistance through Asian Development Bank Trust Funds and are the result of a partnership with the Tbilisi City administration in urban planning and urban transport initiatives. They will guide the gender and disability inclusion work of the ongoing Livable Cities Investment Program to improve planning and infrastructure in major cities and regional clusters in Georgia.

Gathering data to inform the guidelines was sought through a participatory process. To design a local park and recreation area in a low-income residential area, door-to-door interviews and an online questionnaire were conducted to gain community input. The photo below shows local women at a planning meeting at the park scheduled for redevelopment. This was identified as an accessible space where women could bring children and adhere to social distancing. The planning tools catered to all ages and abilities to ensure all the diverse women could identify their preferences and priorities for the park in situ.

Participants provided practical advice to guide a gender and disability-inclusive design for redevelopment. Issues of access, cost, the needs of children and their mothers or carers, persons with disabilities, and older people were all addressed. This included free access to support the development and health of children, elderly people, and persons with disabilities. It specifies that as women are the majority of unpaid carers of children and persons with disabilities, their role as carers needs to be considered in public spaces. To facilitate this, seating is provided near children's play areas and with well-maintained and well-lit disability accessible toilets and refreshment facilities. Safe disability access will be built into the design of paths with street-crossing aids.

The guidelines suggest park activities that are designed for all ages and abilities to ensure an open and inviting space. Inclusive playground features include equipment designed for different physical and developmental disabilities and sensory systems, including sight, touch, and sound. Active play will be catered to through supported swing seats with harnesses, wheelchair accessible roundabouts, wide embankment slides, basket hoops, sand and water tables; with movement, muscle stretching, and mobility enabled though spinning, climbing, sliding, and swinging (which is therapeutic for those with cognitive disabilities). Quiet and more secluded areas will be provided for less confident children and for those experiencing sensory overload (common in girls with autism).

Image description: Local women in Tbilisi sitting and standing around a table in a park conducting an activity as a part of a "street café" (photo by Nana Adeishvili, ADB).

Source: ADB. 2021. *Fair Shared Green and Recreational Spaces Guidelines for Gender-Responsive and Inclusive Design*. Tbilisi Municipality. Manila: ADB. pp. 20–26.

8.6.5 Useful Resources

ADB. 2021. *Fair Shared Green and Recreational Spaces Guidelines for Gender-Responsive and Inclusive Design. Tbilisi Municipality.* Manila: ADB.

These guidelines target priority areas to create a sustainable approach to urban development in Tbilisi, Georgia, ensuring resources are targeted at the areas of most need, while also retaining heritage and greenspace. Sections within the guide look at urban spaces and gardens, principles and steps in gender-responsive and inclusive design of green and recreational spaces, considerations in gender-responsive and inclusive design of green and recreational spaces and standards and criteria for detailed park design. It predominantly focuses on using a gender lens and includes examples of inclusion of women as carers, as well as identifies that good design needs to be disability inclusive as well as gender-responsive and consider the specific needs of persons with disabilities.

ASEAN Australia Smart Cities Trust Fund. 2021. *Gender Equality and Social Inclusion Strategy.* Manila: ADB.

This resource addresses women, persons with disabilities, children, and older people as distinct groups; however, it recognizes intersectionality noting that all categories of disadvantaged groups are not homogenous with the need to acknowledge the different ways that people experience discrimination and exclusion. The strategy considers poverty as a crosscutting issue that exacerbates vulnerabilities and inequalities for all groups of people. The strategy identifies leveraging smart solutions in urban planning, financial management, and service delivery to address the challenges, barriers, and opportunities for women, persons with disabilities, children, and older people through increasing awareness and capacity of city government actors, improving data collection and use through smart solutions, and undertaking analyses and research for city-level smart interventions and improving smart solutions.

ADB. 2022. *Inclusive Cities Urban Area Guidelines.* Manila: ADB.

This set of guidelines for Georgia has been developed to support designers and decision-makers working on new infrastructure projects to create inclusive and livable cities. The resource addresses inclusive urban development, including international and national laws and regulations, universal design (both outdoor and indoor) and accessible tourism development, inclusive urban development and education, and advocacy and public communication. It addresses income inequality, inclusive economic growth, urban rural disparity, unequal access to water, sanitation and energy access, and access to opportunities and participation in society. It addresses gender mainstreaming and intersectionality by identifying the importance of understanding how people experience multiple forms of exclusion and inequality, such as being disabled and being female. It considers an intersectional approach and enables an understanding of how social, cultural, political, and historical contexts can lead to exclusion and inaccessibility in urban settings. It includes separate sections on persons with disabilities, child-friendly and age-friendly cities, as well as an outline of how cities can be safe for women.

S. Fabula and J. Timár. 2018. Violations of the right to the city for women with disabilities in peripheral rural communities in Hungary. *Cities,* Volume 76. pp. 52–57.

This study explores how the right to the city (as a universal human right) applies to rural women who experience multiple social disadvantages. Based on interviews with 32 women with disabilities in rural areas, it analyzes the perceptions of the problems faced by these women in accessing urban resources and services. It was found that the urban–rural divide combined with inequitable and ableist power relations contributed to the violations of the rights of women with disabilities within cities.

Appendix 1: Glossary

Disability Inclusion

Core definitions from the *Convention on the Rights of Persons with Disabilities* (as outlined in section 4.1).

Communication includes languages, display of text, Braille, tactile communication, large print, accessible multimedia, as well as written, audio, plain-language, human-reader, and augmentative and alternative modes, means, and formats of communication, including accessible information and communication technology.

Discrimination on the basis of disability means any distinction, exclusion, or restriction on the basis of disability which has the purpose or effect of impairing or nullifying the recognition, enjoyment or exercise, on an equal basis with others, of all human rights and fundamental freedoms in the political, economic, social, cultural, civil, or any other field. It includes all forms of discrimination, including denial of reasonable accommodation.

Language includes spoken and signed languages and other forms of nonspoken languages.

Reasonable accommodation means necessary and appropriate modification and adjustments not imposing a disproportionate or undue burden, where needed in a particular case, to ensure to persons with disabilities the enjoyment or exercise on an equal basis with others of all human rights and fundamental freedoms.

Universal design means the design of products, environments, programs, and services to be usable by all people, to the greatest extent possible, without the need for adaptation or specialized design. "Universal design" shall not exclude assistive devices for particular groups of persons with disabilities where this is needed.

Additional Definitions Related to Disability

Ableism is a set of beliefs or practices that devalue and discriminate against people with physical, intellectual, or psychiatric disabilities and often rests on the assumption that disabled people need to be "fixed" in one form or the other. Ableism is intertwined in our culture, due to many limiting beliefs about what disability does or does not mean, how able-bodied people learn to treat people with disabilities and how we are often not included at the table for key decisions.[1]

---

[1]   Center for Disability Rights. https://cdrnys.org/blog/uncategorized/ableism/ (accessed 27 February 2023).

Associative discrimination is the legal term that applies when someone is treated unfairly because either someone they know or someone they are associated with has a certain characteristic. For example, it would be associative discrimination if a mother is refused access to an event due to fear of the behavior of her child that has attention deficit hyperactivity disorder (ADHD).[2]

Intersectionality is a concept and theoretical framework that facilitate recognition of the complex ways in which social identities overlap and create compounding experiences of discrimination and concurrent forms of oppression based on two or more grounds, such as gender identity or expression, sex, sexual orientation, ethnicity, caste, descent or inherited status, age, class, disability, or health status.[3]

Twin track approach: The first "track" is the development of specific gender equality and social inclusion activities that target efforts to pilot and/or demonstrate new and emerging ideas that hold potential for significant benefits to women, people with disabilities, and intersectional groups. The second "track" is mainstreaming gender equality and social inclusion (GESI) principles across all initiatives and operations.[4]

Gender

Definitions from ADB's Operations Manual Bank Policies

The approach of the Asian Development Bank (ADB) to gender and development adopts mainstreaming as a key strategy for promoting gender equality and women's empowerment. It defines the key elements of this approach using the following terms:

Gender sensitivity to observe how ADB operations affect women and men differently, and to take into account their different needs and perspectives in planning these operations.

Gender planning to formulate specific strategies that result in equal opportunities and outcomes for women and men.

Gender mainstreaming to ensure that gender concerns and women's needs and perspectives are explicitly considered in all ADB operations, and that women and men participate equally in the decision-making process in development activities.

Agenda setting to assist developing member country governments in formulating strategies to reduce gender disparities and in developing plans and targets for women's and girls' education, health, legal rights, employment, and income earning opportunities.

Source: ADB. 2010. *Operations Manual Bank Policies*. Manila: ADB, p. 1.

---

[2]   Equality, Diversity and Inclusion. University of Cambridge website.
[3]   UN Network on Racial Discrimination and Protection of Minorities. 2022. *Guidance Note on Intersectionality, Racial Discrimination and Protection of Minorities*. Geneva: Office of the High Commissioner for Human Rights. p. 11.
[4]   ASEAN Australia Smart Cities Trust Fund. 2021. *Gender Equality and Social Inclusion Strategy*. Manila: ADB. p. 10.

Additional Definitions Related to Gender

Gender equity refers to the fair distribution of benefits and responsibilities between women and men according to their respective needs. This may involve equal treatment or treatment that is different, but considered equivalent in terms of rights, benefits, and opportunities. In the development context, a gender equity goal may introduce special measures to compensate the disadvantaged women and men, to end inequality and foster autonomy. Gender equity is a process for achieving the goal of gender equality. Gender equality between men and women is a desired outcome or result.[5]

Gender equality means that men and women have the opportunity to develop their full potential and make their own choices free from the limitations set by stereotypes, gender roles, or prejudices. It does not mean that women and men have to become the same, but that their rights, responsibilities, and opportunities will not depend on whether they are born male or female. It means women and men have equal (i) rights under customary or statutory law; (ii) opportunities and access to resources to enhance their human capabilities, productivity, and earnings; and (iii) voice to influence and contribute to the decision-making in governing structures, institutions, and the development process in their communities (footnote 5).

Gender analysis is a systematic approach to understand differences between the development needs and priorities of men and women and the variable impact of development programs on men and women. It uses sex-disaggregated quantitative and qualitative data to understand men's and women's different roles, responsibilities, decision-making power, incentives, and access to productive resources and basic services. Gender analysis includes contextual analysis of the socioeconomic, legal, and political environment as they affect gender-based roles and constraints in society (footnote 5).

Unpaid carer is an individual, such as a family member, neighbor, friend, or other significant individual, who takes on a caring role to support someone with a diminishing physical ability, a debilitating cognitive condition, or a chronic life-limiting illness.[6]

---

[5]   ADB. 2021. *Guidelines for Gender Mainstreaming Categories of ADB Projects*. Manila: ADB. p. 19.

[6]   International Alliance of Carer Organizations (IACO). n.d. Global State of Care. https://internationalcarers.org/wp-content/uploads/2018/11/IACO-EC-GSoC-Report-FINAL-10-20-18-.pdf.

Appendix 2: Types of Violence Experienced by Women and Girls with Disabilities

Type	Definition	Examples
Disability hate crimes[a]	Crimes, typically involving violence, that are motivated by extreme ableism, where the perpetrator targets someone because of their disability.	• Can include any form of violence against a person with disabilities.
Domestic violence (a form of intimate partner violence)	Violence in domestic settings between two people who are, or were, in an intimate relationship.	• Can involve any of the other forms described in this table (e.g., physical, sexual, emotional, psychological, or financial abuse).
Family violence	A broader term than domestic violence as it extends to violence between family members (including e.g., elder abuse, adolescent violence against parents, or violence from co-residents).	• Can involve any of the other forms described in this table (e.g., physical, sexual, emotional, psychological, or financial abuse).
Financial abuse	Limiting or removing someone's access to their money or controlling their financial decisions.	• Withholding money (including government pensions) for necessities like food, medication. or disability-related equipment. • Not allowing access to debit and/or credit cards. • Abusing access to a personal identification number (PIN) when helping a woman with disabilities manage her bank account. • Limiting access to employment.
Intimate partner violence	Violence within current or past intimate relationships (including marriages, de facto relationships, and other intimate relationships between people who may or may not live together).	• Can involve any of the other forms described in this table (e.g., physical, sexual, emotional, psychological, or financial abuse).
Medical exploitation or abuse	Acts, treatments, and procedures that interfere with the autonomy of a person to make decisions about their health.	• Forced or coerced psychiatric interventions (e.g., electroconvulsive therapy). • Withholding of, or forced, medication or medical intervention.
Neglect	Depriving a person of the necessities of life such as food, water, shelter, clothing, medical care, or education, either willfully or passively.	• Withholding or delaying personal care or access to disability-related equipment. • Tampering with medication or mobility or communication devices. • Denying that someone needs the supports they say they need.

Type	Definition	Examples
Physical violence	Behavior that intentionally harms a person's body.	• Punching, hitting, slapping, kicking, strangling. Note: Physical violence can also be directed toward the assistance animals of people with disabilities.
Psychological or emotional abuse	Behavior that aims to cause emotional or psychological harm.	• Verbal aggression. • Coercive control—a pattern of abusive, coercive, and intimidating behavior that aims to dominate and control someone, causing them to feel controlled, overpowered, and scared. Can include physical, financial, emotional, or psychological behaviors (e.g., gaslighting). • Humiliation, regularly putting someone down to damage their self-worth. • Stalking (repeated contact, harassment, threats, tracking, or spying). • Threats, e.g., of violence, institutionalization, withdrawing care, having children removed, harming pets, assistance animals, or family members. • Denying or trivializing the experience of disability. • Isolating a person or preventing them from seeing certain people. • Denying, revealing, or threatening to reveal someone's gender identity or sexuality.
Restrictive practices	Practices or interventions that restrict the rights or freedom of movement of a person with disabilities.	• Physical restraint—a person using their body to restrain someone. • Mechanical restraint—using equipment to restrain someone. • Chemical restraint—using drugs or medicines to restrain or control someone. • Seclusion—putting a person in a room or space they cannot leave either because the exit is locked or barred, or because there are real or perceived consequences for leaving. • Environmental restraint—preventing or restricting someone's access to the community, areas of their homes (including fridges or cupboards), or personal possessions (including disability aids).
Sexual and reproductive coercion or violence	Acts, treatments, and procedures that interfere with the autonomy of a person to make decisions about their sexual and reproductive health.	• Reproductive coercion (including forced or coerced pregnancy). • Forced abortion, contraception, or sterilization. • Withholding contraception.
Sexual harassment	Any unwelcome conduct of a sexual nature which makes a person feel offended, humiliated, and/or intimidated, where a reasonable person would anticipate that reaction in the circumstances.	• Unwelcome sexual advances or requests for sexual favors. • Suggestive comments or innuendo. • Unwanted text messages, e-mail, or contact via social media that is sexual in nature (including photographs).
Sexual violence/ assault	Sexual activity that happens where consent is not obtained or freely given. It occurs any time a person is forced, coerced, or manipulated into any sexual activity.	• Rape. • Sexual assault. • Unwanted sexual touch. • Forced marriage.

Type	Definition	Examples
Spiritual and cultural abuse	Using spiritual or religious ideas or beliefs to hurt, scare, or control someone.	• Not allowing a person to practice their beliefs or customs. • Forcing someone to practice beliefs or customs which they do not believe in.
Technology facilitated abuse	Using technology to harass, threaten, monitor, control, impersonate, or intimidate.	• Sending nude or embarrassing images of a person to others without consent. • Removing or limiting access to a means of communication.

a   Organisation for Security and Cooperation in Europe, Office for Democratic Institutions and Human Rights. n.d. *Hate crime against people with disabilities.*

Source: Our Watch and Women with Disabilities Victoria. 2022. *Changing the Landscape: A National Resource to Prevent Violence Against Women and Girls with Disabilities.* Melbourne, Australia: Our Watch, pp. 28–31.

References

Amin, A. S., M. A. A. Razak, and N. M. Akhir. 2021. Access to Transportation: The Experiences of Women with Physical Disabilities. *International Journal of Academic Research in Business and Social Sciences*, 11(6). pp. 883–890.

ASEAN Australia Smart Cities Trust Fund. 2021. *Gender Equality and Social Inclusion Strategy*. Manila: ADB. https://www.adb.org/documents/aasctf-gender-equality-social-inclusion-strategy.

Asian Development Bank (ADB). 2013. *Tool Kit on Gender Equality Results and Indicators*. Manila: ADB. https://www.adb.org/documents/tool-kit-gender-equality-results-and-indicators.

ADB. 2018. *Strategy 2030: Achieving a Prosperous, Inclusive, Resilient, and Sustainable Asia and the Pacific*. Manila: ADB.

ADB. 2019. *The Social Protection Indicator for the Pacific: Assessing Progress*. Manila: ADB. https://www.adb.org/sites/default/files/publication/513481/spi-pacific-2019.pdf.

ADB. 2020. *Gender Equality and Social Inclusion Diagnostic of Selected Sectors in Nepal*. Manila: ADB.

ADB. 2020. *Women's Time Use in Rural Tajikistan*. Manila: ADB.

ADB. 2021. *Disability and Social Protection in Asia*. ADB Briefs, No. 203. Manila: ADB.

ADB. 2021. *Fair Shared Green and Recreational Spaces Guidelines for Gender-Responsive and Inclusive Design*. Tbilisi Municipality. Manila: ADB. https://www.adb.org/publications/green-spaces-guidelines-gender-responsive-design-tbilisi.

ADB. 2022. *Gender Equality and Social Inclusion Diagnostic of Selected Sectors in Nepal October 2020*. Manila: ADB. https://www.adb.org/sites/default/files/publication/646661/nepal-gender-equality-social-inclusion-diagnostic.pdf.

ADB. 2022. *Good Practice Note on Addressing Sexual Exploitation, Abuse, and Harassment in ADB-Financed Projects with Civil Works*. Manila: ADB.

ADB. 2022. *Inclusive Cities Urban Area Guidelines*. Manila: ADB. https://www.adb.org/publications/inclusive-cities-urban-area-guidelines.

Astbury, J. 2001. Gender disparities in mental health. *Mental Health. Ministerial Round Tables 2001, 54th World Health Assembly*. Geneva: WHO.

Blyth, J., K. Alexander, and L. Woolf. 2020. *Out of the Margins: An intersectional analysis of disability and diverse sexual orientation, gender identity, expression and sex characteristics in humanitarian and development contexts*. Canberra: DFAT.

Braunmiller, J. C., and M. Dry. 2022. *The Importance of Designing Gender and Disability Inclusive Laws: A Survey of Legislation in 190 Economies. Global Indicators Briefs 11 (12 September)*. World Bank, Washington, DC.

CBM. 2016. *Inclusion Counts: The Economic Case for Disability-Inclusive Development*. Bensheim, Germany: CBM.

CBM. 2019. *Leave No One Behind: Gender Equality, Disability Inclusion and Leadership for Sustainable Development*. Melbourne: CBM. p. 3.

Centre for Advocacy and Research. 2020. *Sexual and Gender Minorities and COVID-19: Guidance for WASH Delivery*. Delhi: CFAR.

Clifton, S. 2020. *Research Report Hierarchies of power: Disability theories and models and their implications for violence against, and abuse, neglect, and exploitation of, people with disability*. Canberra: Royal Commission into violence, abuse, neglect and exploitation of people with disability. https://disability.royalcommission.gov.au/system/files/2020-10/Research%20Report%20-%20 Hierarchies%20of%20power_Disability%20theories%20and%20models%20and%20their%20 implications%20for%20violence%20against%2C%20and%20abuse%2C%20neglect%2C%20and%20 exploitation%20of%2C%20people%20with%20disability.pdf.

The Cooperative Research Centre for Water Sensitive Cities. 2022. Urban Water Guide. Canberra: Australian Water Partnership.

DFAT. 2015. *Development for All 2015–2020: Strategy for strengthening disability-inclusive development in Australia's aid program*. Canberra: DFAT.

DFAT. 2021. *Disability Inclusion in the DFAT Development Program Good Practice Note*. Canberra: DFAT. https://www.dfat.gov.au/sites/default/files/disability-inclusive-development-guidance-note.pdf.

DFAT. n.d. *Accessibility Design Guide: Universal design principles for Australia's aid program*. Canberra: DFAT. https://www.dfat.gov.au/about-us/publications/Pages/accessibility-design-guide-universal-design-principles-for-australia-s-aid-program.

Dilli, D. 1997. *Handbook: Accessibility and Tool Adaptations for Disabled Workers in Post Conflict and Developing Countries*. Geneva: ILO. https://www.ilo.org/wcmsp5/groups/public/---ed_emp/---ifp_skills/documents/publication/wcms_107950.pdf.

Disability Inclusive and Accessible Urban Development Network, CBM. 2016. *The Inclusion Imperative: Towards Disability-inclusive and Accessible Urban Development Key Recommendations for an Inclusive Urban Agenda*. Berkeley: World Enabled.

Fabula, S. and J. Timár. 2018. Violations of the right to the city for women with disabilities in peripheral rural communities in Hungary. *Cities,* Volume 76. pp. 52–57. https://www.sciencedirect.com/science/article/abs/pii/S0264275116302281.

FCDO Disability Inclusion and Rights Strategy 2022–2030. *Building an Inclusive Future for All: A Sustainable Rights Based Approach February 2022.* London: The Foreign, Commonwealth and Development Office. https://assets.publishing.service.gov.uk/government/uploads/system/uploads/attachment_data/file/1074127/ Disability-Inclusion-and-Rights-Strategy-2022.pdf.

Gan, S. W. et al. 2022. *Entrepreneurship Training and Online Marketplace Participation among Female Persons with Disabilities.* ADBI Working Paper 1342. Tokyo: Asian Development Bank Institute. https://www.adb.org/sites/default/files/publication/836491/adbi-wp1342.pdf.

GSMA. 2020. *The Digital Exclusion of Women with Disabilities: A Study of Seven Low- and Middle-Income Countries.* London: GSMA. https://www.gsma.com/mobilefordevelopment/wp-content/uploads/2020/07/GSMA_Digital-Exclusion-of-Women-with-Disabilities_44pp_ACCESSIBLE.pdf.

Inclusion London. 2015. *Factsheet: The Social Model of Disability*. London: Inclusion London. https://www.inclusionlondon.org.uk/wp-content/uploads/2015/05/FactSheets_TheSocialModel.pdf.

Indigenous Persons with Disabilities Global Network. 2022. *Indigenous women with disabilities: a path towards inclusion and collaboration in 2021.* https://www.iwgia.org/en/indigenous-persons-with-disabilities-global-network-ipwdgn/4702-iw-2022-ipwdgn.html.

Inter-American Development Bank. 2019. *Goodbye Barriers! Guide for the design of more accessible spaces.* J. L. Borau Jordán, J. de Moraes Pinheiro, S. Duryea. https://gdlab.iadb.org/en/findability_ui/results/publications/diversity/entrepreneurship.

International Disabilities Alliance. 2022. *The Global Disability Summit 2022 Report.* New York: IDA. https://www.internationaldisabilityalliance.org/sites/default/files/gds_report_2022_norad.pdf.

International Disabilities Alliance, Indigenous Peoples with Disabilities Global Network, and UN Women. 2020. *Fact Sheet: Indigenous Women with Disabilities.* New York: IDA.

Iudici, A., L. Bertoli, and E. Faccio. 2017. The "invisible" needs of women with disabilities in transportation systems. *Crime Prevention and Community Safety.* September. pp. 264–275.

International Labour Organization (ILO). 2018. *Care Work and Care Jobs for the Future of Decent Work.* Geneva: ILO.

Jolly, J. 2022. Organisations want to recruit more women with autism, dyslexia and ADHD to work in cybersecurity roles. *The Guardian.* https://www.theguardian.com/society/2022/nov/16/neurodiverse-women-sought-for-jobs-at-gchq-and-bae-systems (accessed 17 November 2022).

Kothari, M. 2005. *Women and adequate housing: Study by the Special Rapporteur on adequate housing as a component of the right to an adequate standard of living.* New York: UN Commission on Human Rights Sixty-first session. https://digitallibrary.un.org/record/543365?ln=en.

London School of Hygiene and Tropical Medicine. 2020. *Water, Women and Disability Study: Main Report.* Canberra: DFAT.

Mcclain-Nhlapo, C. V. et al. 2020. *Pivoting to Inclusion: Leveraging Lessons from the COVID-19 Crisis for Learners with Disabilities.*

Mehrotra, N. 2006. Negotiating Gender and Disability in Rural Haryana. *Sociological Bulletin.* Vol. 55, No. 3. pp. 406–426.

Ministry of Public Works, Timor-Leste. 2017. *Social Safeguards Framework for Rural Road Works.* Dili: Roads for Development Programme, Ministry of Public Works, Timor-Leste, and the ILO. https://www.ilo.org/dyn/asist/docs/F-1213814048/SOCIAL%20SAFEGUARDS%20FRAMEWORK%20for%20Rural%20Road%20Work.pdf.

OECD. 2009. *Cognitive Impairment, Mental Health and Transport: Design with Everyone in Mind.* Paris: OECD and International Transport Forum.

Ortoleva, S. 2015. Yes, Girls and Women with Disabilities Do Math! An Intersectionality Analysis. A. Hans. ed. *Disability, Gender and the Trajectories of Power.* Thousand Oaks, California: Sage Publishing.

Our Watch and Women with Disabilities Victoria. 2022. *Changing the landscape: A national resource to prevent violence against women and girls with disabilities.* Melbourne, Australia: Our Watch.

Pacific Disability Forum. 2014. *Toolkit on Eliminating Violence Against Women and Girls with Disabilities in Fiji.* Suva: DFAT. https://miusa.globaldisabilityrightsnow.org/wp-content/uploads/2016/01/Toolkit-on-Eliminating-Violence-Against-Women-And-Girls-With-Disabilities-In-Fiji-_1_-1.pdf.

Pacific Women Shaping Pacific Development. 2021. *Thematic Brief: Inclusion of Pacific Women with Disabilities.* Canberra: DFAT.

Research Excellence in Disability and Health. 2020. *Intimate partner violence against people with disability in Australia.* Melbourne: Melbourne Disability Institute.

Scherer, N. et al. 2021. The Inclusion of Rights of People with Disabilities and Women and Girls in Water, Sanitation, and Hygiene Policy Documents and Programs of Bangladesh and Cambodia: Content Analysis Using EquiFrame. *Int. J. Environ. Res. Public Health, 18.* p. 5087.

Social Protection Approaches to COVID-19: Expert Advice (SPACE). 2020. *Inclusive Information Systems for Social Protection: Intentionally Integrating Gender and Disability.* London: FCDO, GIZ, and DFAT. https://reliefweb.int/report/world/space-inclusive-information-systems-social-protection-intentionally-integrating-gender.

SPACE. 2020. *Strengthening Gender Equality and Social Inclusion (GESI) During the Implementation of Social Protection Responses to COVID-19.* London: FCDO and GIZ. https://socialprotection.org/discover/publications/space-strengthening-gender-equality-and-social-inclusion-gesi-during.

Starkey, P. and J. Hine. 2014. *Poverty and sustainable transport How transport affects poor people with policy implications for poverty reduction.* Nairobi: UN-Habitat and the Overseas Development Institute (ODI). https://sustainabledevelopment.un.org/content/documents/1767Poverty%20and%20sustainable%20transpo rt.pdf.

Szalavitz, M. 2016. Autism—It's Different in Girls: New research suggests the disorder often looks different in females, many of whom are being misdiagnosed and missing out on the support they need. https://www.scientificamerican.com/article/autism-it-s-different-in-girls/. 27(2): pp. 48–55.

Tovaas, K. 2020. How to make inclusive mobility a reality: 8 principles and tools for a fair(er) transport system. Brussels: European Commission. http://www.h2020-inclusion.eu/fileadmin/user_upload/Documents/Deliverables/inclusion_D3.4_publication_fin_web.pdf.

UN ESCAP. 1995. *Hidden Sisters: Women and Girls with Disabilities in the Asian and Pacific Region.* Bangkok: ESCAP,

UN ESCAP. 2018. *Building Disability-Inclusive Societies in Asia and the Pacific: Assessing Progress of the Incheon Strategy.* Bangkok: ESCAP. https://www.unescap.org/sites/default/files/publications/SDD%20BDIS%20report%20A4%20v14-5-E.pdf.

UN Habitat. 2012. *Gender Issue Guide Urban Planning and Design.* Nairobi: UN Habitat.

UN Habitat. 2022. *Cities for Girls Cities for All.* Nairobi: Habitat.

UN Girls Education Initiative and Leonard Cheshire. 2017. *Still left behind: Pathways to inclusive education for girls with disabilities.* New York: UNGEI.

UN Women. 2014. *Ensuring Safe Transport with and for Women and Girls in Port Moresby.* Papua New Guinea: UN Women. https://unwomen.org.au/wp-content/uploads/2015/12/UNW_safe_public_transport.pdf.

UN Women. 2017. *Issue Brief: Making the SDGs Count for Women and Girls with Disabilities.* New York: UN Women.

UN Women. 2018. *Gender Accessibility Audit Toolkit.* New York: UN Women and the National Assembly of People with Disabilities in Ukraine. https://eca.unwomen.org/sites/default/files/Field%20Office%20ECA/Attachments/Publications/2019/gender-accessibility-audit-ENG_compressed.pdf.

UN Women. 2019. *Issues Brief: Making the SDGs Count for Women and Girls with Disabilities.* New York: UN Women.

UN Women. 2020. *Addressing Exclusion through Intersectionality in Rule of Law, Peace and Security Context.* New York: UN Women.

UN Women. 2020. *Safe Cities and Safe Public Spaces for Women and Girls Global Flagship Initiative: Second International Compendium of Practices.* New York: UN Women. https://www.unwomen.org/en/digital-library/publications/2020/02/safe-cities-and-safe-public-spaces-international-compendium-of-practices-2.

UN Women. 2021. *Accessibility Audit Brief.* New York: UN Women. https://www.unwomen.org/sites/default/files/Headquarters/Attachments/Sections/Library/Publications/2021/ Brief-Accessiblity-audit-en.pdf.

UN Women. 2021. *Experiences of Women with Disabilities in the Asia-Pacific Region during COVID-19.* New York: UN Women. https://www.unwomen.org/sites/default/files/2022-01/Brief-Experiences-of-women-with-disabilities-in-the-Asia-Pacific-region-during-COVID-19-en_0.pdf.

UN Women. 2022. *Assessment of the Needs of Women and Girls with Disabilities and the State of Protection of their Rights in Georgia.* Tbilisi: UN Women.

UN Women. 2022. *Progress on the Sustainable Development Goals: The Gender Snapshot 2022.* New York: UN Women.

UN Women and Sightsavers. 2021. *"This virus has changed us all": Experiences of women with disabilities in the Asia-Pacific region during COVID-19.* New York: UN Women.

UNFPA. 2018. *Women and Young Persons with Disabilities Guidelines for Providing Rights-Based and Gender-Responsive Services to Address Gender-Based Violence and Sexual and Reproductive Health and Rights.* New York: UNFPA. https://womenenabled.org/reports/wei-and-unfpa-guidelines-disability-gbv/.

UNFPA. 2021. *COVID-19, Gender, and disability checklist: Ensuring Human Rights-Based Sexual and Reproductive Health for Women, Girls, and Gender Non-conforming Persons with Disabilities during the COVID-19 Pandemic.* Bangkok: UNFPA.

UNFPA, Women Enabled International, and Pacific Disability Forum. 2021. *Women and young people with disabilities in Samoa: Needs assessment of sexual and reproductive health and rights, gender-based violence, and access to essential services.* Apia, Samoa: UNFPA.

UNFPA, Women Enabled International, and Pacific Disability Forum. 2022. *Women, Girls, and Gender Non-Conforming People with Disabilities — Know Your Rights! Gender-based violence and sexual and reproductive health during the COVID-19 pandemic in the Pacific Region.* Fiji: UNFPA.

UNICEF. 2021. *Seen, Counted, included: Using data to shed light on the well-being of children with disabilities.* New York: UNICEF.

United Nations. 2016. *New Urban Agenda.* New York: Habitat III Secretariat.

United Nations. 2018. *Disability and Development Report Realizing the Sustainable Development Goals by, for and with Persons with Disabilities.* New York: UN Department of Economic and Social Affairs.

United Nations. 2018. *Incheon Strategy to "Make the right real" for persons with disabilities in Asia and the Pacific and Beijing Declaration and including the Action Plan to accelerate the implementation of the Incheon Strategy.* New York: Economic and Social Commission for Asia and the Pacific.

United Nations. 2020. Policy Brief no. 69: *Leaving no one behind: the COVID-19 crisis through the disability and gender lens.* New York: UN United Nations Department of Economic and Social Affairs. https://www.un.org/development/desa/dpad/wp-content/uploads/sites/45/publication/PB_69.pdf.

United Nations. 2020. *Sixth session of the Working Group on the Asian and Pacific Decade of Persons with Disabilities, 2013–2022: Review of recent progress in the implementation of the Asian and Pacific Decade of Persons with Disabilities, 2013–2022.* Bangkok: UN Economic and Social Commission for Asia and the Pacific.

United Nations. 2020. *World Population Ageing 2020 Highlights: Living Arrangements of Older Persons.* New York: Department of Economic and Social Affairs, Population Division.

United Nations and ADB. 2019. *Accelerating progress: An empowered, inclusive and equal Asia and the Pacific.* Bangkok: UN ESCAP.

United Nations Committee on the Elimination of Discrimination against Women. 2010. *General recommendation No. 27 on older women and protection of their human rights.*

United Nations Committee on the Rights of the Child Forty-third session. 2006. *General Comment No. 9 (2006): The rights of children with disabilities.* New York: UN.

United Nations Convention on the Rights of Persons with Disability General Comment No. 3. 2016.: Women and Girls with Disabilities.

United Nations General Assembly. 2017. Resolution A/RES/72/162. *Implementation of the Convention on the Rights of Persons with Disabilities and the Optional Protocol.* New York: UNGA. n1745519.pdf (un.org)

United Nations General Assembly Sixty-seventh session. 2012. Report of the Special Rapporteur on Violence against Women, its Causes and Consequences.

USAID. 2020. *Guide on How to Integrate Disability into Gender Assessments and Analyses.* Washington, DC: USAID.

Water Aid. 2017. Gender Equality and Disability Inclusion within Water, Sanitation and Hygiene: Exploring integrated Approaches to Addressing Inequality. Melbourne: WaterAid. https://www.wateraid.org/au/sites/g/files/jkxoof231/files/2017-12/Gender%20equality%20and%20disability%20inclusion%20in%20WASH.pdf.

Water for Women. 2019. *Disability Inclusive Systems Strengthening in WASH: How can we do it better?* Canberra: DFAT.

Women Enabled International. 2013. Statement at the UN Commission on the Status of Women, 57th session, 8 March 2013. *Harmful Traditional Practices and Violence Against Women and Girls with Disabilities.* Washington, DC: WEI.

Women Enabled International. 2017. *Comments on Draft CEDAW General Recommendation on Gender Related Dimensions of Disaster Risk Reduction in a Changing Climate.* Washington, DC: WEI.

Women Enabled International. 2018. *Facts: The Sexual and Reproductive Health and Rights of Women and Girls with Disabilities.* Washington, DC: WEI.

Women Enabled International. 2019. *Submission by Women Enabled International and Disability Rights International to the Committee on the Elimination of Discrimination Against Women on its Elaboration of a General Recommendation on Trafficking in Women and Girls in the Context of Global Migration.* Washington, DC: WEI.

Women Enabled International. 2021. *Factsheet: The Right to Education for Women and Girls with Disabilities.* Washington, DC: WEI.

Women's Refugee Commission. 2015. *Including Adolescent Girls with Disabilities in Humanitarian Programs: Principles and Guidelines.* New York: WRC.

World Bank. 2010. Mainstreaming *Gender in Road Transport: Operational Guidance for World Bank Staff.* Washington, DC: World Bank.

World Bank. 2017. *Including Persons with Disabilities in Water Sector Operations: A Guidance Note.* Washington, DC: The World Bank.

World Bank. 2018. *Disability Inclusion and Accountability Framework.* Washington, DC: World Bank.

World Bank. 2019. *Brief on Violence Against Women and Girls with Disabilities.* Washington, DC: World Bank, The Global Women's Institute, Inter-American Bank, and the International Center for Research on Women.

World Bank. 2019. *Equity and Inclusion in Education in World Bank Projects: Persons with Disabilities, Indigenous Peoples, and Sexual and Gender Minorities.* Washington, DC: World Bank. https://www.inclusive-education-initiative.org/knowledge-repository/equity-and-inclusion-education-world-bank-projects-persons-disabilities.

World Bank. 2020. *Pivoting to Leveraging Lessons from the COVID-19 Crisis for Learners with Disabilities.* Washington, DC: World Bank.

World Bank. 2020. *World Bank Handbook for Gender-Inclusive Urban Planning and Design.* Washington, DC: World Bank. https://www.worldbank.org/en/topic/urbandevelopment/publication/handbook-for-gender-inclusive-urban-planning-and-design.

World Bank. 2022. *Charting a Course towards Universal Social Protection: Resilience, Equity, and Opportunity for All.* Washington. DC: World Bank. https://reliefweb.int/report/world/charting-course-towards-universal-social-protection-resilience-equity-and-opportunity-all-enarzh.

World Bank. 2022. *Global Indicators Briefs No. 11: The Importance of Designing Gender and Disability Inclusive Laws: A Survey of Legislation in 190 Economies.* Washington, DC: World Bank.

World Health Organization. 2014. *Eliminating forced, coercive and otherwise involuntary sterilization: An interagency statement OHCHR, UN Women, UNAIDS, UNDP, UNFPA, UNICEF, and WHO.* Geneva: WHO.

World Health Organization. 2019. *Disability Factsheet Sustainable Development Goals: Health Targets.* Geneva: WHO.

World Health Organization. 2022. *Abuse of Older People.* https://www.who.int/news-room/fact-sheets/detail/abuse-of-older-people.

World Health Organization and the World Bank. 2011. *World Report on Disability.* Geneva: WHO.

World Vision Vanuatu and International Centre for Evidence in Disability at the London School of Hygiene and Tropical Medicine. 2020. *Water, Women and Disability Study Main Report.* Canberra: DFAT.

www.ingramcontent.com/pod-product-compliance
Lightning Source LLC
Chambersburg PA
CBHW040250290326
41929CB00058B/3500